Responsive Layouts

Flex, Grid & Multi-Column

Abdelfattah Ragab

Responsive Layouts

Flex, Grid and Multi-Column

Abdelfattah Ragab

Introduction

Welcome to the book "Responsive Layouts: Flex, Grid and Multi-Column"

In this book I explain the three best-known responsive layouts: the Flexbox, the Grid and the Multi-Column layout.

Flexbox is a one-dimensional layout that only works in one dimension at a time, either horizontally or vertically.

The grid layout is a two-dimensional layout that distributes the elements horizontally and vertically at the same time.

The multi-column layout is a special layout for magazines and newspapers, where the text should flow in columns with spacing, rules, etc.

I'll explain all the properties and their values and how they affect the distribution of elements on the screen.

So let's get started.

Flexbox

Flexbox is a one-dimensional layout that works with one dimension at a time.

To use the flexbox layout, simply set the display property to flex or inline-flex as follows:

display: flex; or display: inline-flex;

If you set the display to flex, it is a block element, if you set it to inline-flex, it is an inline element. This is exactly the same as setting display to block or inline. And what about flex?

The flex influences how the subordinate elements should be distributed on the page.

So we have the flex container, the element with display: flex;

And we have the flex elements, the children of the flex container;

All properties that you apply to the container also affect the subordinate elements.

The container has its own properties and the children have their own properties and here's a quick overview of them all.

The container properties

- `display`: flex or display: inline-flex: Specifies that the container is a flex container and its children are flex items.
- `flex-direction`: Defines the direction of the main axis, which determines how flex items are positioned. Values can be row, row-reverse, column, or column-reverse.
- `justify-content`: Aligns flex items along the main axis. It controls the spacing between and around the flex items. Values include flex-start, flex-end, center, space-between, space-around, and space-evenly.
- `align-items`: Aligns flex items along the cross axis (perpendicular to the main axis). It controls how flex items are distributed vertically. Values can be flex-start, flex-end, center, baseline, or stretch.
- `flex-wrap`: Specifies whether flex items should wrap to multiple lines when they exceed the width of the flex container. Values include nowrap, wrap, and wrap-reverse.

- `align-content:` Defines the alignment of flex lines when there is extra space on the cross axis. It applies to multi-line flex containers. Values can be flex-start, flex-end, center, space-between, space-around, or stretch.
- `gap:` Defines the space between the flex elements

The Item properties

- `flex-grow:` Specifies the ability of a flex item to grow to fill available space. It determines how the remaining space is distributed among flex items. Default value is 0.
- `flex-shrink:` Specifies the ability of a flex item to shrink if necessary when the flex container is too small. Default value is 1.
- `flex-basis:` Specifies the initial size of a flex item before it's distributed in the flex container. Values can be a length, a percentage, or auto.
- `flex:` Shorthand for flex-grow, flex-shrink, and flex-basis.
- `order:` Defines the order in which flex items are displayed. Lower values appear first. Default value is 0.

- `align-self:` Overrides the align-items property for a specific flex item. It allows you to align an item along the cross axis independently. Values can be auto, flex-start, flex-end, center, baseline, or stretch.

Example

We have 5 div elements with different sizes and colors as follows. By setting display flex in their wrapper, they are displayed as follows:

```
<style>
  .wrapper {
    display: flex;
  }
  .div-1 {
    width: 100px;
```

```css
  height: 160px;
  background-color: magenta;
}
.div-2 {
  width: 60px;
  height: 170px;
  background-color: blue;
}


.div-3 {
  width: 100px;
  height: 180px;
  background-color: green;
}
.div-4 {
  width: 100px;
  height: 120px;
  background-color: brown;
}
.div-5 {
  width: 120px;
  height: 160px;
  background-color: orange;
}
```

```html
</style>
<div class="wrapper">
  <div class="div-1"></div>
  <div class="div-2"></div>
  <div class="div-3"></div>
  <div class="div-4"></div>
  <div class="div-5"></div>
</div>
```

Before applying display flex to the wrapper, they looked like this

Now let's understand how flex layout works.

Flex layout has two main axes, the main axis and the cross axis

The main axis is defined by the flex-direction property, and the cross axis is perpendicular to it.

flex-direction can have four values: row, column, row-reverse and column-reverse.

if flex-direction is not specified, it is set to row by default

flex-direction

The flex-direction property specifies the direction of the flexible elements.

If the element is not a flexible element, the flex-direction property has no effect.

Values

- row
- row-reverse
- column
- column-reverse

row

Default value. The flexible items are displayed horizontally, as a row

```css
.wrapper {
  display: flex;
  flex-direction: row;
}
```

Same as row, but in reverse order

```
.wrapper {
  display: flex;
  flex-direction: row-reverse;
```

```
}
```

column

The flexible items are displayed vertically, as a column

```css
.wrapper {
  display: flex;
  flex-direction: column;
}
```

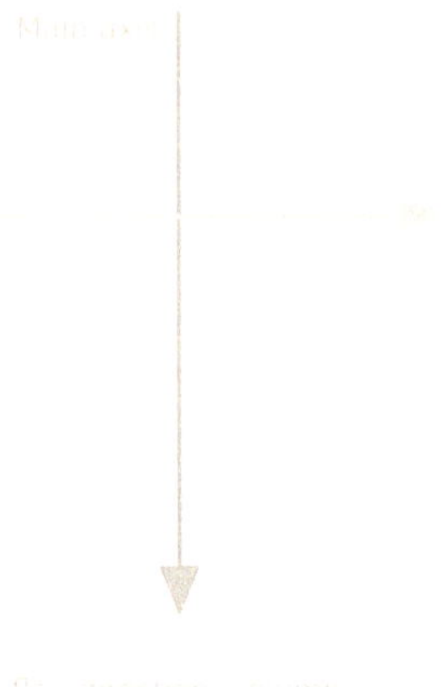

column-reverse

Same as column, but in reverse order

```css
.wrapper {
  display: flex;
```

```
    flex-direction: column-reverse;
}
```

Now let's look at how you can benefit from this, starting
with two important flex layout properties justify-content
and align-items.
I will explain the flex direction of the row in detail and
leave it to you to try the other flex directions

justify-content

The CSS property justify-content determines how the
browser distributes the space between and around
content elements along the main axis of a flex container

Values

- flex-start
- flex-end
- center
- space-between
- space-around
- space-evenly

Let's explain each value and see it in action

I'll start with the default value, flex-start

flex-start

Default value. Items are positioned at the beginning of
the container

```
.wrapper {
```

```css
  display: flex;
  flex-direction: row;
  justify-content: flex-start;
}
```

flex-end

Items are positioned at the end of the container

```css
.wrapper {
  display: flex;
  flex-direction: row;
  justify-content: flex-end;
}
```

It is aligned at the end of the flex container to the right of the screen. You must note that there is a difference between flex-direction: row-reversed and justify-content: flex-end;

They are not the same thing. Justify-content is about alignment, i.e. it keeps the same order and aligns it to the end of the flex container. In the case of flex-direction: row-reverse, the main axis is reversed and so is the order.

center

Items are positioned in the center of the container

```
.wrapper {
  display: flex;
  flex-direction: row;
  justify-content: center;
}
```

space-between

Items will have space between them

```
.wrapper {
  display: flex;
  flex-direction: row;
  justify-content: space-between;
}
```

space-around

Items will have space before, between, and after them

```
.wrapper {
  display: flex;
  flex-direction: row;
  justify-content: space-around;
}
```

space-evenly

Items will have equal space around them

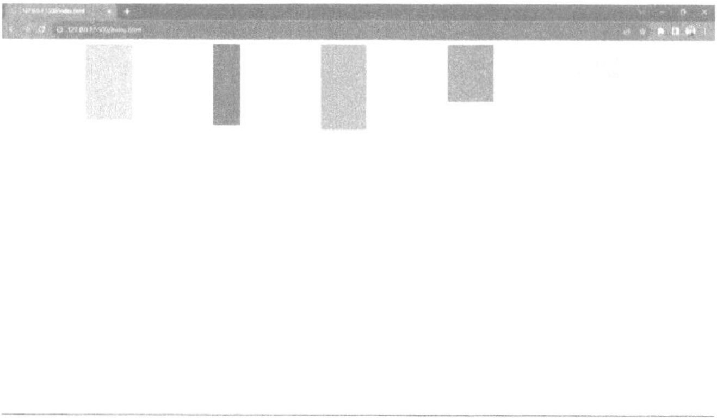

```css
.wrapper {
  display: flex;
  flex-direction: row;
  justify-content: space-evenly;
}
```

That was for the main axis, now let's see how we can align the elements on the cross axis with the align-items property

align-items

Controls the alignment of items on the Cross Axis.

Values

- normal
- stretch

- center
- flex-start
- flex-end
- baseline

Let's explain each value and see it in action

I'll start with the default value, normal or stretch

normal or stretch (same behavior)

Items are stretched to fit the container

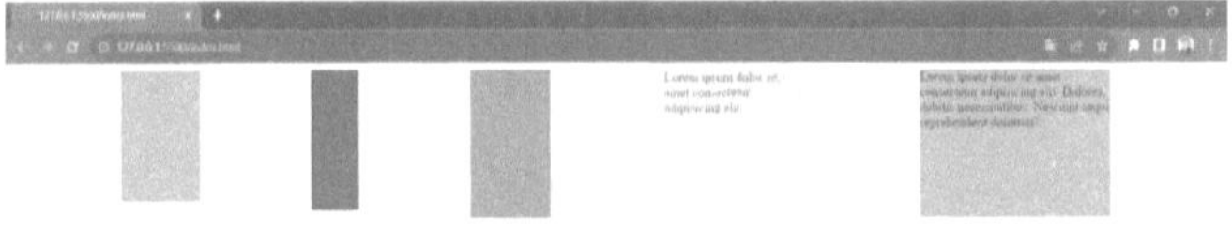

```
<style>
  .wrapper {
    display: flex;
    flex-direction: row;
    justify-content: space-evenly;
```

```css
  align-items: stretch;
}
.div-1 {
  width: 100px;
  height: 160px;
  background-color: magenta;
}
.div-2 {
  width: 60px;
  height: 170px;
  background-color: blue;
}


.div-3 {
  width: 100px;
  height: 180px;
  background-color: green;
}
.div-4 {
  width: 180px;
  height: auto;
  background-color: mediumspringgreen;
}
.div-5 {
```

```html
      width: 240px;
      height: auto;
      background-color: orangered;
    }
</style>
<div class="wrapper">
  <div class="div-1"></div>
  <div class="div-2"></div>
  <div class="div-3"></div>
  <div class="div-4">
    Lorem ipsum dolor sit, amet
consectetur adipisicing elit.
  </div>
  <div class="div-5">
    Lorem ipsum dolor sit amet
consectetur adipisicing elit. Dolores,
debitis
    necessitatibus. Nesciunt sequi
reprehenderit dolorum?
  </div>
</div>
```

The last two div elements now expand to fill the entire
height of the container

center

Items are positioned at the center of the container

```css
.wrapper {
  display: flex;
  flex-direction: row;
  justify-content: space-evenly;
  align-items: center;
}
```

flex-start

Items are positioned at the beginning of the container

```
.wrapper {
  display: flex;
  flex-direction: row;
  justify-content: space-evenly;
  align-items: flex-start;
}
```

flex-end

Items are positioned at the end of the container

```
.wrapper {
  display: flex;
  flex-direction: row;
  justify-content: space-evenly;
  align-items: flex-end;
}
```

baseline

Items are positioned at the baseline of the container

```
.wrapper {
  display: flex;
  flex-direction: row;
  justify-content: space-evenly;
  align-items: baseline;
}
```

Have you considered what happens when we have many div elements that exceed the width of the container?
There is a flex property that handles this case. It is called flex-wrap

flex-wrap

The CSS property flex-wrap determines whether flex elements are forced into one line or can wrap into multiple lines.

To better understand this, I want to increase the number of div elements on the page so that they no longer fit on one line.

Values

- nowrap
- wrap
- wrap-reverse

nowrap

Default value. Specifies that the flexible items will not wrap

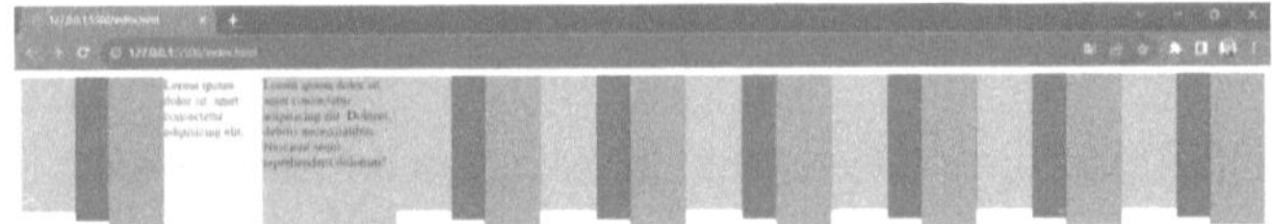

```
<style>
  .wrapper {
    display: flex;
    flex-direction: row;
    flex-wrap: nowrap;
  }
  .div-1 {
    width: 100px;
    height: 160px;
    background-color: magenta;
  }
  .div-2 {
    width: 60px;
    height: 170px;
    background-color: blue;
  }
```

```css
    .div-3 {
      width: 100px;
      height: 180px;
      background-color: green;
    }
    .div-4 {
      width: 180px;
      height: auto;
      background-color: mediumspringgreen;
    }
    .div-5 {
      width: 240px;
      height: auto;
      background-color: orangered;
    }
```
```html
</style>
<div class="wrapper">
  <div class="div-1"></div>
  <div class="div-2"></div>
  <div class="div-3"></div>
  <div class="div-4">
    Lorem ipsum dolor sit, amet
consectetur adipisicing elit.
```

```html
    </div>
    <div class="div-5">
        Lorem ipsum dolor sit amet
consectetur adipisicing elit. Dolores,
debitis
        necessitatibus. Nesciunt sequi
reprehenderit dolorum?
    </div>
    <div class="div-1"></div>
    <div class="div-2"></div>
    <div class="div-3"></div>
    <div class="div-1"></div>
    <div class="div-2"></div>
    <div class="div-3"></div>
    <div class="div-1"></div>
    <div class="div-2"></div>
    <div class="div-3"></div>
    <div class="div-1"></div>
    <div class="div-2"></div>
    <div class="div-3"></div>
    <div class="div-1"></div>
    <div class="div-2"></div>
    <div class="div-3"></div>
    <div class="div-1"></div>
```

```html
  <div class="div-2"></div>
  <div class="div-3"></div>
</div>
```

The div elements have been shrunk to fit the width of the container. This happens because of the flex property flex-shrink, which has a default value of 1, which means that the elements should be shrunk to fit into the container.

I will disable this property for now to see the actual behavior of the elements without flex-shrink. Deactivate it by setting the value to 0;

flex-shrink is a property for the flex element and not for the flex container, i.e. it must be set for each flex element in the flex container.

In the flex layout, we have the flex container that we have worked with so far and which we have marked with the .wrapper class.

And we have flex elements that are div elements of div-1, div-2,... etc.

We will discuss the flex elements and their properties soon, but first let's understand flex-wrap and now disable flex-shrink for all flex elements

Select all div elements within the .wrapper and deactivate the flex-shrink property

```
.wrapper div {
  flex-shrink: 0;
}
```

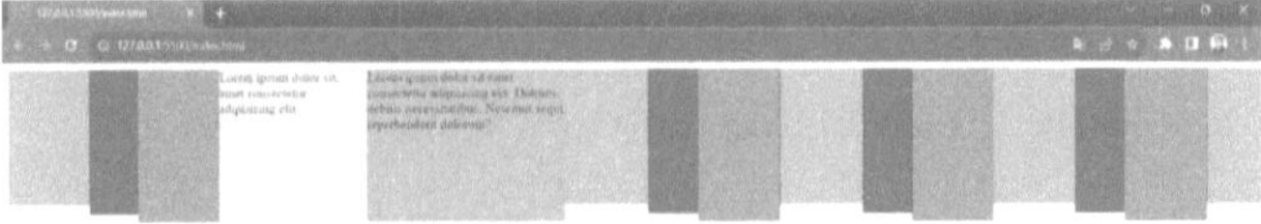

As you can see, the elements have retained their original size, but now we have a scrollbar at the bottom of the page

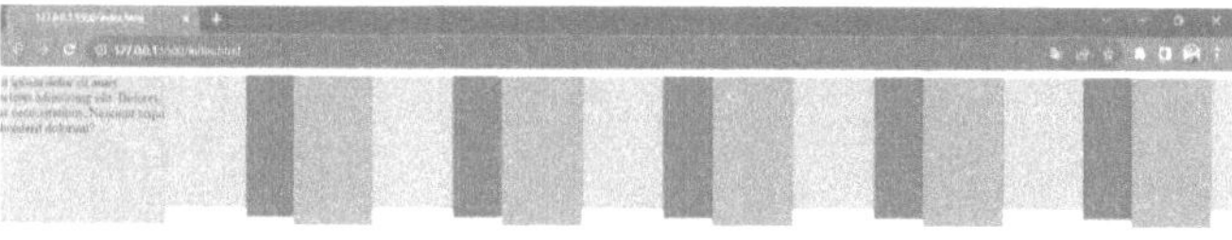

wrap

Specifies that the flexible items will wrap if necessary
Now we will see how the elements within the flex
container are wrapped by setting the flex-wrap property
to the value wrap

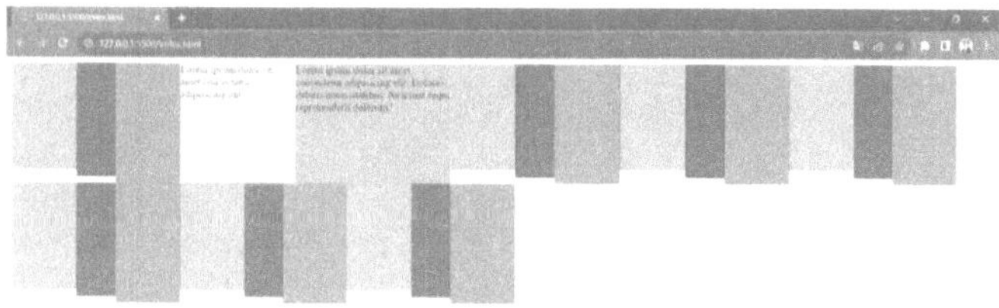

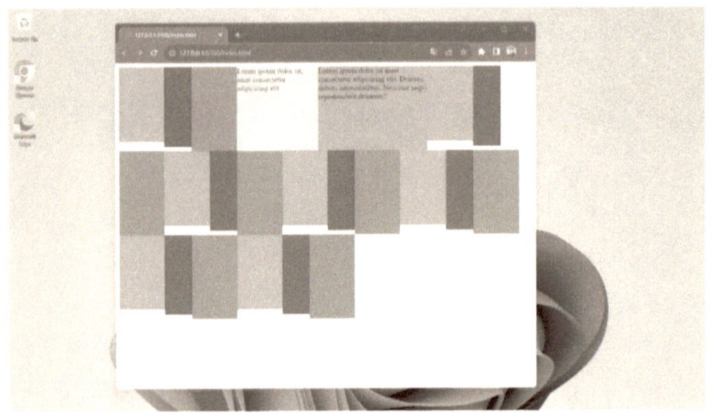

```
.wrapper {
  display: flex;
  flex-direction: row;
  flex-wrap: wrap;
}
```

To make it clearer, I number all div elements

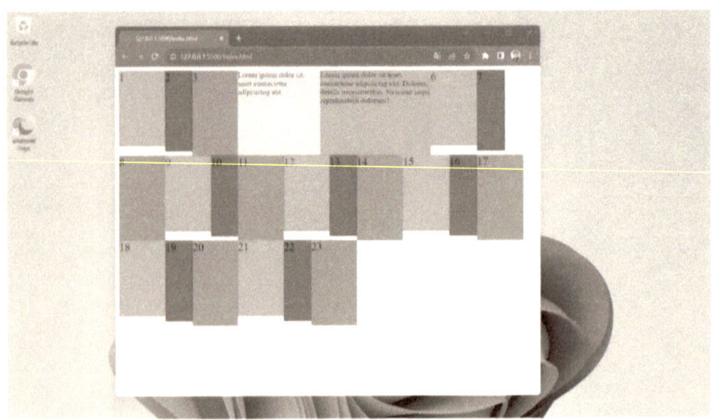

```
<style>
```

```css
.wrapper {
  display: flex;
  flex-direction: row;
  flex-wrap: wrap;
}
.wrapper div {
  flex-shrink: 0;
}
.div-1 {
  width: 100px;
  height: 160px;
  background-color: magenta;
  font-size: 24px;
}
.div-2 {
  width: 60px;
  height: 170px;
  background color: blue;
  font-size: 24px;
}

.div-3 {
  width: 100px;
  height: 180px;
```

```css
      background-color: green;
      font-size: 24px;
    }
    .div-4 {
      width: 180px;
      height: auto;
      background-color: mediumspringgreen;
    }
    .div-5 {
      width: 240px;
      height: auto;
      background-color: orangered;
    }
</style>
<div class="wrapper">
  <div class="div-1">1</div>
  <div class="div-2">2</div>
  <div class="div-3">3</div>
  <div class="div-4">
    Lorem ipsum dolor sit, amet
consectetur adipisicing elit.
  </div>
  <div class="div-5">
```

Lorem ipsum dolor sit amet
consectetur adipisicing elit. Dolores,
debitis
    necessitatibus. Nesciunt sequi
reprehenderit dolorum?
</div>
<div class="div-1">6</div>
<div class="div-2">7</div>
<div class="div-3">8</div>
<div class="div-1">9</div>
<div class="div-2">10</div>
<div class="div-3">11</div>
<div class="div-1">12</div>
<div class="div-2">13</div>
<div class="div-3">14</div>
<div class="div-1">15</div>
<div class="div-2">16</div>
<div class="div 3">17</div>
<div class="div-1">18</div>
<div class="div-2">19</div>
<div class="div-3">20</div>
<div class="div-1">21</div>
<div class="div-2">22</div>
<div class="div-3">23</div>

```
</div>
```

wrap-reverse

Specifies that the flexible elements should be wrapped
in reverse order.

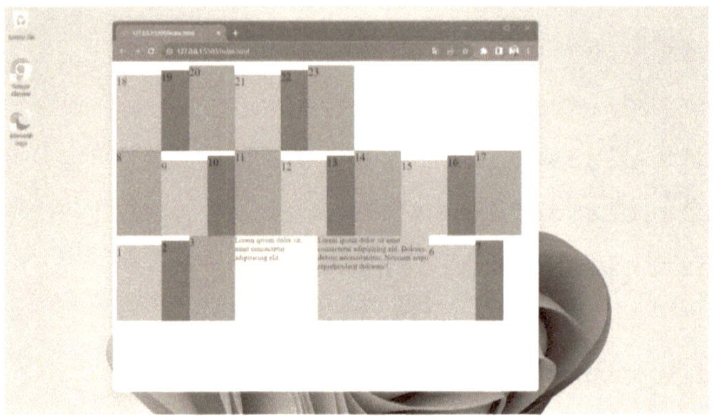

```
.wrapper {
    display: flex;
    flex-direction: row;
    flex-wrap: wrap-reverse;
}
```

gap

The gap property defines the size of the gap between
the rows and between the columns in flexbox, grid or

multi-column layout. It is a shorthand for the following properties: row-gap and column-gap

Values

- <row-gap> <column-gap>

row-gap column-gap

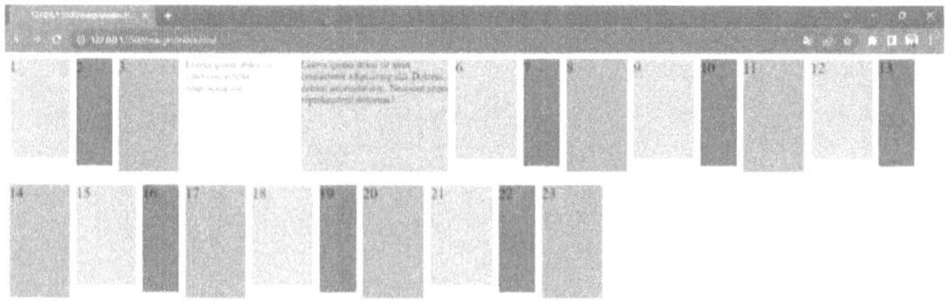

```
.wrapper {
  display: flex;
  flex-direction: row;
  flex-wrap: wrap;
  gap: 20px 10px;
}
```

align-content

The align-content property determines how the flex lines are distributed along the transverse axis in a flexbox container.

It only works if your flex elements extend over several lines and there is therefore a space between the lines. It has no effect if the elements are only in one line.

Values

- stretch
- center
- flex-start
- flex-end
- space-between
- space-around
- space-evenly

stretch

Default value. Lines stretch to take up the remaining space

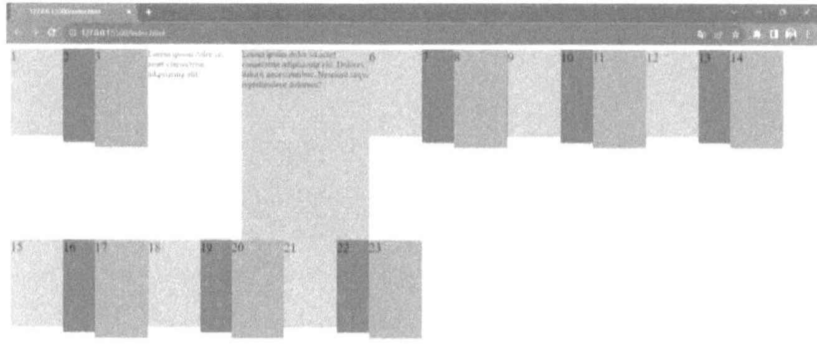

```css
.wrapper {
  display: flex;
  flex-direction: row;
  flex-wrap: wrap;
  height: 700px;
  background-color: lightblue;
  align-content: stretch;
}
```

center

Lines are packed toward the center of the flex container

```css
.wrapper {
  display: flex;
  flex-direction: row;
  flex-wrap: wrap;
  height: 700px;
  background-color: lightblue;
  align-content: center;
}
```

flex-start

Lines are packed toward the start of the flex container

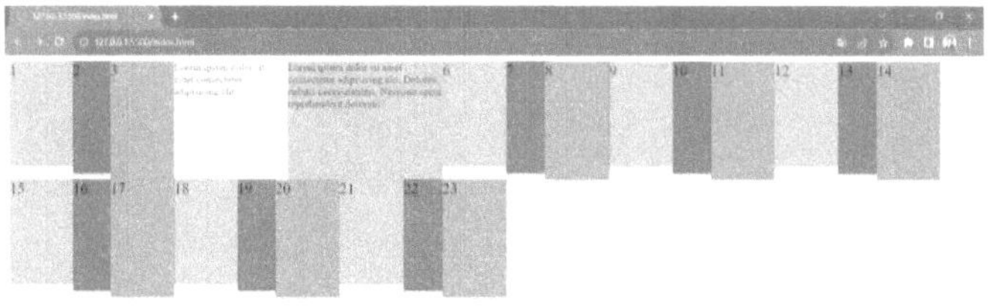

```css
.wrapper {
  display: flex;
  flex-direction: row;
  flex-wrap: wrap;
  height: 700px;
  background-color: lightblue;
  align-content: flex-start;
}
```

flex-end

Lines are packed toward the end of the flex container

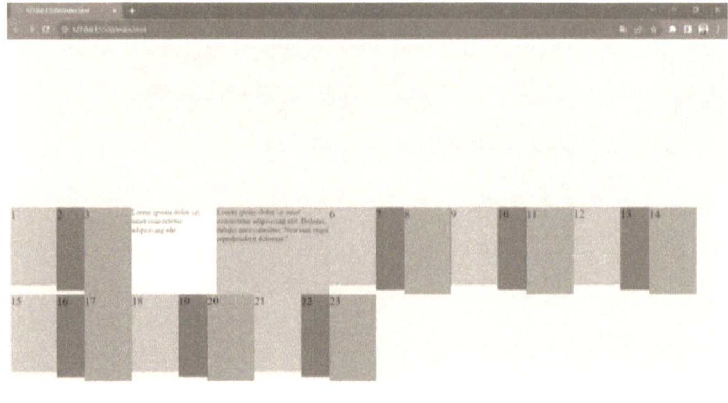

```css
.wrapper {
  display: flex;
  flex-direction: row;
  flex-wrap: wrap;
  height: 700px;
  background-color: lightblue;
  align-content: flex-end;
}
```

space-between

Lines are evenly distributed in the flex container

```
.wrapper {
  display: flex;
  flex-direction: row;
  flex-wrap: wrap;
  height: 700px;
  background-color: lightblue;
  align-content: space-between;
}
```

space-around

Lines are evenly distributed in the flex container, with half-size spaces on either end

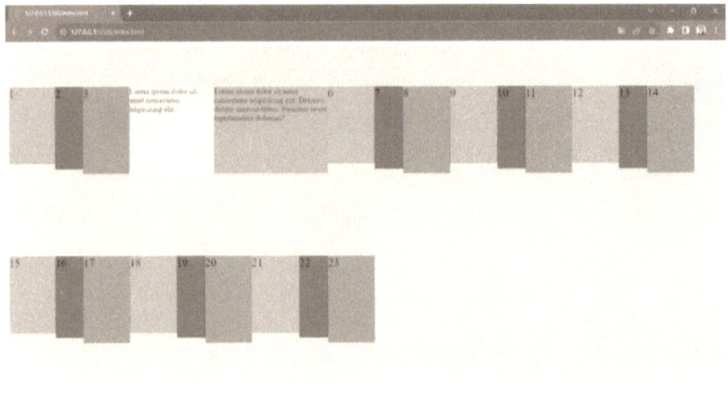

```css
.wrapper {
  display: flex;
  flex-direction: row;
  flex-wrap: wrap;
  height: 700px;
  background-color: lightblue;
  align-content: space-around;
}
```

space-evenly

Lines are evenly distributed in the flex container, with equal space around them

```css
.wrapper {
  display: flex;
  flex-direction: row;
  flex-wrap: wrap;
  height: 700px;
  background-color: lightblue;
  align-content: space-evenly;
}
```

You can combine other properties, such as, row-gap, column-gap, gap, align-items…etc.

column-gap and align-items

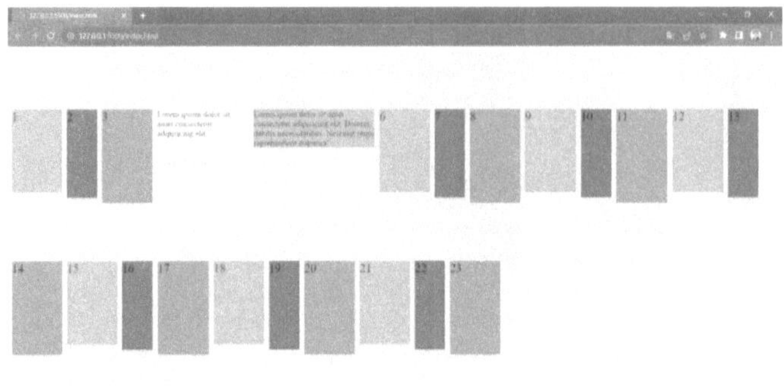

```css
.wrapper {
  display: flex;
  flex-direction: row;
  flex-wrap: wrap;
  height: 700px;
  background-color: lightblue;
  align-content: space-evenly;
  column-gap: 10px;
  align-items: flex-start;
}
```

Now that we have looked at the properties of the flex container, let's explain the properties of the flex elements.

Flex Item Properties

The direct subordinate elements of a flex container automatically become flex elements.

In our examples, the .wrapper div element is the flex container and all subordinate div elements such as .div-1, .div-2, ... etc. are the flex elements.

The flex item properties are defined individually for each one

flex-grow

The flex-grow property specifies how much the item will grow relative to the rest of the flexible items inside the same container.

Values

- number

number

I will apply flex-grow to the blue div, .div-2

```css
<style>
  .wrapper {
    display: flex;
    flex-direction: row;
    flex-wrap: wrap;
  }
  .div-1 {
    width: 100px;
```

```css
  height: 160px;
  background-color: magenta;
  font-size: 24px;
}
.div-2 {
  width: 60px;
  height: 170px;
  background-color: blue;
  font-size: 24px;
  flex-grow: 1;
}


.div-3 {
  width: 100px;
  height: 180px;
  background-color: green;
  font-size: 24px;
}
.div-4 {
  width: 180px;
  height: auto;
  background-color: mediumspringgreen;
}
.div-5 {
```

```css
    width: 240px;
    height: auto;
    background-color: orangered;
  }
```

```html
</style>
<div class="wrapper">
  <div class="div-1">1</div>
  <div class="div-2">2</div>
  <div class="div-3">3</div>
  <div class="div-4">
    Lorem ipsum dolor sit, amet
consectetur adipisicing elit.
  </div>
  <div class="div-5">
    Lorem ipsum dolor sit amet
consectetur adipisicing elit. Dolores,
debitis
    necessitatibus. Nesciunt sequi
reprehenderit dolorum?
  </div>
</div>
```

grow .div-3

Now I will also let the green div .div-3 grow

```css
.div-3 {
  width: 100px;
  height: 180px;
  background-color: green;
  font-size: 24px;
  flex-grow: 1;
}
```

You can determine how much everyone should grow. I will give the blue div a value of 3

```css
.div-2 {
  width: 60px;
  height: 170px;
  background-color: blue;
  font-size: 24px;
  flex-grow: 3;
}
.div-3 {
  width: 100px;
  height: 180px;
  background-color: green;
  font-size: 24px;
  flex-grow: 1;
}
```

flex-shrink

The flex-shrink property determines how the element shrinks in relation to the other flexible elements in the same container.

Values

- number

number

Update .div-2 so that it shrinks 4x more than other elements.

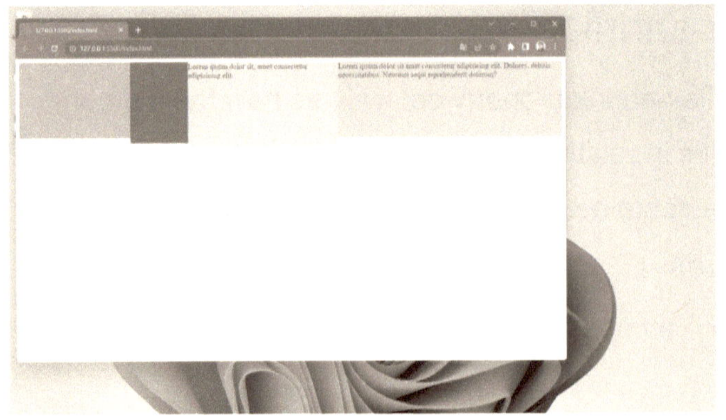

```
<style>
  .wrapper {
    display: flex;
    flex-direction: row;
    flex-wrap: nowrap;
  }
  .div-1 {
    width: 300px;
    height: 160px;
    background-color: magenta;
  }
  .div-2 {
    width: 500px;
    height: 170px;
    background-color: blue;
    flex-shrink: 4;
```

```css
      }
    .div-3 {
      width: 400px;
      height: 180px;
      background-color: lightpink;
    }
    .div-4 {
      width: 600px;
      height: 160px;
      background-color: orange;
    }
</style>
<div class="wrapper">
  <div class="div-1"></div>
  <div class="div-2"></div>
  <div class="div-3">
    Lorem ipsum dolor sit, amet
consectetur adipisicing elit.
  </div>
  <div class="div-4">
    Lorem ipsum dolor sit amet
consectetur adipisicing elit. Dolores,
debitis
```

```
        necessitatibus. Nesciunt sequi
reprehenderit dolorum?
    </div>
</div>
```

prevent shrink

To prevent an element from shrinking, set its value to 0.

flex-shrink: 0

I will prevent the first div element from shrinking

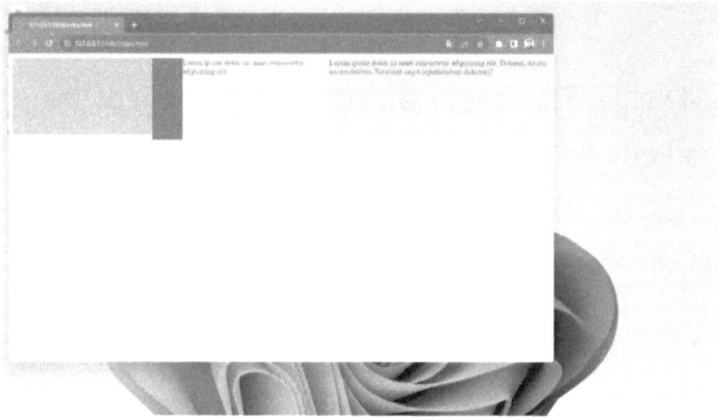

```css
.div-1 {
  width: 300px;
  height: 160px;
  background-color: magenta;
  flex-shrink: 0;
}
```

flex-basis

The flex-basis property defines the initial length of a flex element.flex-basis has a higher priority than width or height (if set).

Values

- auto
- number

auto

Default value. The length is equal to the length of the flexible item. If the item has no length specified, the length will be according to its content.

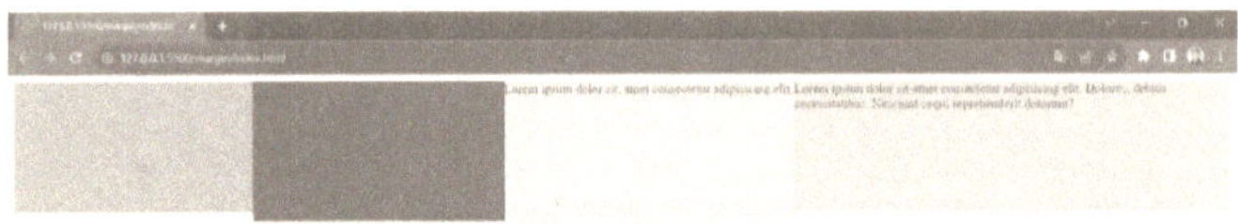

```
.div-1 {
    width: 300px;
    height: 160px;
    background-color: magenta;
    flex-shrink: 0;
    flex-basis: auto;
}
```

number

A length unit, or percentage, specifying the initial length of the flexible item(s)

```
.div-1 {
  width: 300px;
  height: 160px;
  background-color: magenta;
  flex-shrink: 0;
  flex-basis: 600px;
}
```

flex

The flex property is a shorthand property for:

flex: <flex-grow>< flex-shrink> <flex-basis>

Values

- flex-grow flex-shrink flex-basis
- auto
- none

flex-grow flex-shrink flex-basis

Initial value is

flex: 0 1 auto

One value

1. <flex-grow>. In the case of a value, this is assigned to the <flex-grow>.
2. <flex-basis>. If it is not a valid value for the <flex-grow>, it is assigned to the <flex-basis>

Two values

1. <flex-grow>. The first value must be a valid value for the <flex-grow> while the second value is assigned first to <flex-shrink> if possible.
2. <flex-basis>. Otherwise it will be assigned to <flex-basis>

Three values

1. <flex-grow> <flex-shrink> <flex-basis>.

order

The order property specifies the order of a flexible item relative to the rest of the flexible items inside the same container.

The elements are arranged visually according to their order number, lowest values first.

Values

- number

It's not only about ordering elements, but also about grouping elements.

You can use the order property to group elements.

Here is an example, we have some div elements like this

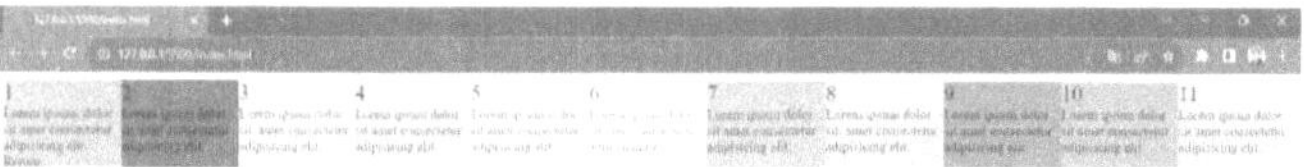

```
<style>
  .wrapper {
```

```css
  display: flex;
  flex-direction: row;
  flex-wrap: nowrap;
}
.wrapper div {
  width: 160px;
  height: 100px;
}
.wrapper div span {
  display: block;
  font-size: 25px;
}
.div-1 {
  background-color: magenta;
}
.div-2 {
  background-color: blue;
}
.div-3 {
  background-color: lightpink;
}
.div-4 {
  background-color: orange;
}
```

```css
    .div-5 {
      background-color: lightgreen;
    }
    .div-6 {
      background-color: antiquewhite;
    }
    .div-7 {
      background-color: cornflowerblue;
    }
    .div-8 {
      background-color: darkturquoise;
    }
    .div-9 {
      background-color: darkorchid;
    }
    .div-10 {
      background-color: mediumpurple;
    }
    .div-11 {
      background-color: sandybrown;
    }
</style>
<div class="wrapper">
  <div class="div-1">
```

```html
    <span>1</span>
    Lorem ipsum, dolor sit amet
consectetur adipisicing elit. Rerum.
  </div>
  <div class="div-2">
    <span>2</span>
    Lorem ipsum dolor sit amet
consectetur adipisicing elit.
  </div>
  <div class="div-3">
    <span>3</span>
    Lorem ipsum dolor sit, amet
consectetur adipisicing elit.
  </div>
  <div class="div-4">
    <span>4</span>
    Lorem ipsum dolor sit amet
consectetur adipisicing elit.
  </div>
  <div class="div-5">
    <span>5</span>
    Lorem ipsum dolor sit amet
consectetur adipisicing elit.
  </div>
```

```html
  <div class="div-6">
    <span>6</span>
    Lorem ipsum dolor sit amet
consectetur adipisicing elit.
  </div>
  <div class="div-7">
    <span>7</span>
    Lorem ipsum dolor sit amet
consectetur adipisicing elit.
  </div>
  <div class="div-8">
    <span>8</span>
    Lorem ipsum dolor sit, amet
consectetur adipisicing elit.
  </div>
  <div class="div-9">
    <span>9</span>
    Lorem ipsum dolor sit amet
consectetur adipisicing elit.
  </div>
  <div class="div-10">
    <span>10</span>
    Lorem ipsum dolor sit amet
consectetur adipisicing elit.
```

```
</div>
<div class="div-11">
  <span>11</span>
  Lorem ipsum dolor sit amet
consectetur adipisicing elit.
  </div>
</div>
```

number

Now, let's group 6 and 7 together.

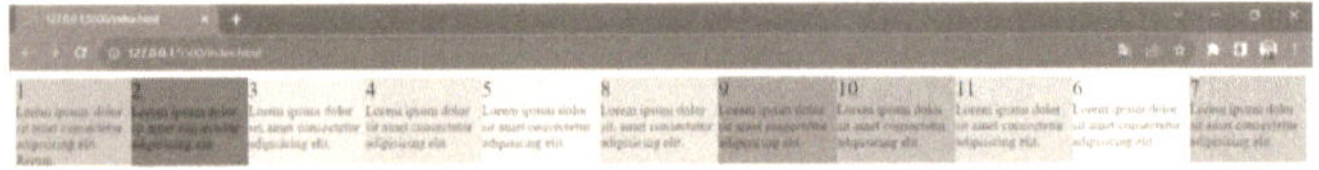

```
.div-6 {
  background-color: antiquewhite;
  order: 1;
}
.div-7 {
```

```css
    background-color: cornflowerblue;
    order: 1;
}
```

negative number

Flex items have a default order value of 0.

Now set order to -1;

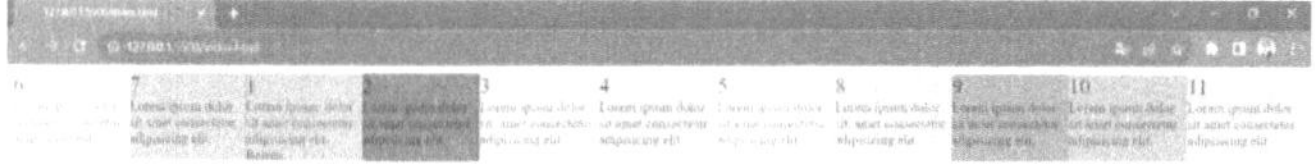

```css
.div-6 {
    background-color: antiquewhite;
    order: -1;
}
.div-7 {
    background-color: cornflowerblue;
    order: -1;
```

}

You can group and order elements using the flex order property

Note that the order property, like all flex properties, only works for flex layouts. If the element is not a flexible element, the order property has no effect.

The last property we are going to discuss here is the align-self.

align-self

The CSS property align-self overrides the value align-items of a flex element.

The align-self property is set per element in order to apply an alignment that differs from the alignment of the container for all elements.

It accepts the same values as align-items, but again, it only works for the element, not the container.

Values

- auto
- stretch
- center
- flex-start
- flex-end

- baseline

Here is an example. We have many div elements inside a container that has align-items: flex-end;
Now, I will apply align-self to .div-5 and .div-6

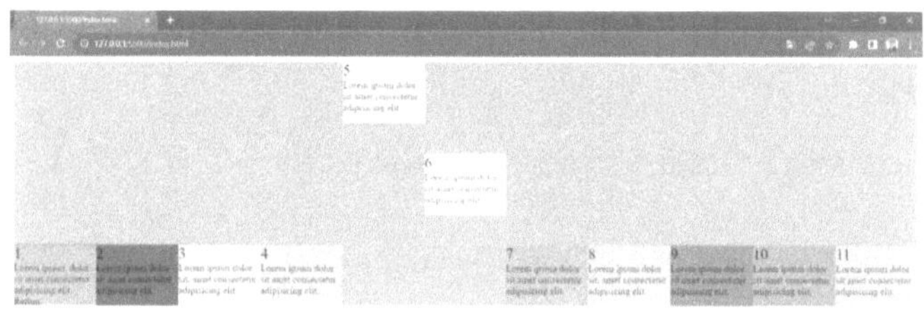

```
<style>
  .wrapper {
    display: flex;
    flex-direction: row;
    flex-wrap: nowrap;
    height: 400px;
    background-color: lightseagreen;
    align-items: flex-end;
  }
  .wrapper div {
    width: 160px;
```

```css
    height: 100px;
}
.wrapper div span {
  display: block;
  font-size: 25px;
}
.div-1 {
  background-color: magenta;
}
.div-2 {
  background-color: blue;
}
.div-3 {
  background-color: lightpink;
}
.div-4 {
  background-color: orange;
}
.div-5 {
  background-color: lightgreen;
  align-self: flex-start;
}
.div-6 {
  background-color: antiquewhite;
```

```css
      align-self: center;
    }
    .div-7 {
      background-color: cornflowerblue;
    }
    .div-8 {
      background-color: darkturquoise;
    }
    .div-9 {
      background-color: darkorchid;
    }
    .div-10 {
      background-color: mediumpurple;
    }
    .div-11 {
      background-color: sandybrown;
    }
</style>
<div class="wrapper">
  <div class="div-1">
    <span>1</span>
    Lorem ipsum, dolor sit amet
consectetur adipisicing elit. Rerum.
  </div>
```

```html
<div class="div-2">
  <span>2</span>
  Lorem ipsum dolor sit amet
consectetur adipisicing elit.
</div>
<div class="div-3">
  <span>3</span>
  Lorem ipsum dolor sit, amet
consectetur adipisicing elit.
</div>
<div class="div-4">
  <span>4</span>
  Lorem ipsum dolor sit amet
consectetur adipisicing elit.
</div>
<div class="div-5">
  <span>5</span>
  Lorem ipsum dolor sit amet
consectetur adipisicing elit.
</div>
<div class="div-6">
  <span>6</span>
  Lorem ipsum dolor sit amet
consectetur adipisicing elit.
```

```html
    </div>
    <div class="div-7">
      <span>7</span>
      Lorem ipsum dolor sit amet
consectetur adipisicing elit.
    </div>
    <div class="div-8">
      <span>8</span>
      Lorem ipsum dolor sit, amet
consectetur adipisicing elit.
    </div>
    <div class="div-9">
      <span>9</span>
      Lorem ipsum dolor sit amet
consectetur adipisicing elit.
    </div>
    <div class="div-10">
      <span>10</span>
      Lorem ipsum dolor sit amet
consectetur adipisicing elit.
    </div>
    <div class="div-11">
      <span>11</span>
```

```
    Lorem ipsum dolor sit amet
consectetur adipisicing elit.
  </div>
</div>
```

Now we've covered everything to do with the flex layout.

By utilizing these features, you can create complex and responsive layouts with ease. I encourage you to experiment and combine different flexbox properties to achieve the layout you want for your website.

Grid Layout

CSS3 Grid Layout is a powerful two-dimensional layout system that allows you to create grid-based layouts on web pages. It provides precise control over the placement and alignment of elements within a grid container. Here is an overview of CSS3 Grid Layout and its key concepts:

Container properties

- `display:` Defines the element as a grid container. Values: grid or inline-grid.

- `grid-template-columns`: Defines the track sizes for the grid's columns. Values: a space-separated list of <length>, <percentage>, or <fr> units.
- `grid-template-rows`: Defines the track sizes for the grid's rows. Values: a space-separated list of <length>, <percentage>, or <fr> units.
- `grid-template-areas`: Defines a grid template by referencing the names of the grid areas.
- `grid-auto-columns`: Defines the size of implicitly created columns. Values: a space-separated list of <length>, <percentage>, or <fr> units.
- `grid-auto-rows`: Defines the size of implicitly created rows. Values: a space-separated list of <length>, <percentage>, or <fr> units.
- `grid-auto-flow`: Defines how auto-placed items get flowed into the grid. Values: row, column, row dense, or column dense.

- `column-gap:` Defines the size of the gap between columns.
- `row-gap:` Defines the size of the gap between rows.
- `gap:` A shorthand for setting both grid-row-gap and grid-column-gap.

Item properties

- `grid-column-start:` Specifies a grid item's start position within the grid column.
- `grid-column-end:` Specifies a grid item's end position within the grid column.
- `grid-row-start:` Specifies a grid item's start position within the grid row.
- `grid-row-end:` Specifies a grid item's end position within the grid row.
- `grid-column:` A shorthand for setting both grid-column-start and grid-column-end.
- `grid-row:` A shorthand for setting both grid-row-start and grid-row-end.
- `grid-area:` A shorthand for setting grid-row-start, grid-column-start, grid-row-end, and grid-column-end in one declaration.

- `justify-self`: Aligns the grid item along the inline (row) axis.
- `align-self`: Aligns the grid item along the block (column) axis.
- `place-self`: A shorthand for setting both justify-self and align-self.

Grid tracks are the columns and rows that make up the grid layout.

By default, tracks are created automatically based on the content and size of the grid items.

You can also explicitly define tracks using properties like grid-template-columns and grid-template-rows.

We have an example with some div elements like this

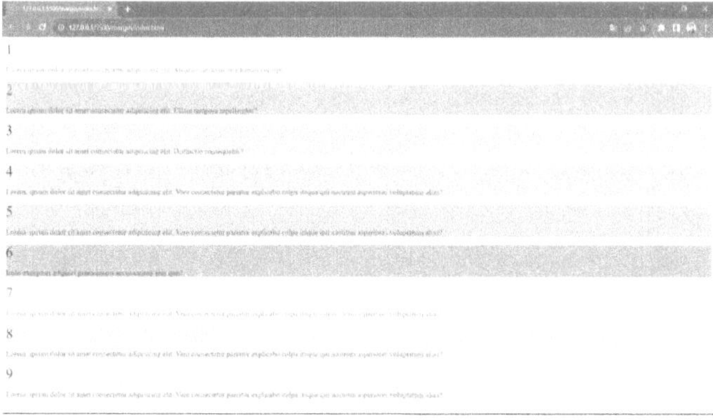

The space around the elements is set by the browser by default, and you can remove it by using the universal selector as follows

```css
* {
    margin: 0;
    padding: 0;
}
```

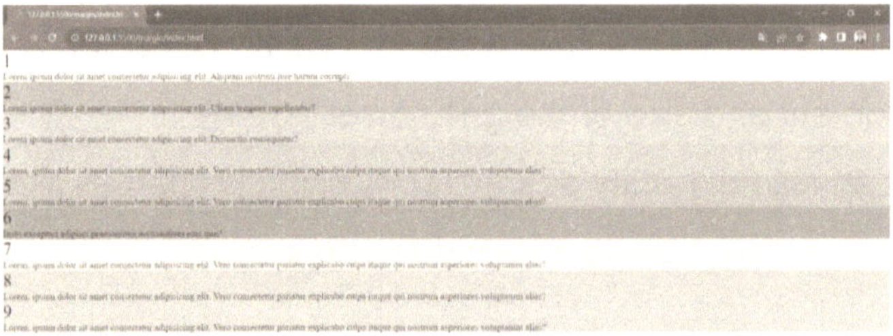

To make this a grid layout, I will set display: grid; to the container,

```css
.wrapper {

  display: grid;

}
```

Now it is a grid layout, but it has no columns defined.

grid-template-columns

The grid-template-columns property defines the number (and width) of columns in a grid layout.

The values are a space-separated list in which each value specifies the size of the respective column.

Values

- none
- auto
- max-content
- min-content

- length

Default value. Columns are created if needed

```html
<style>
  * {
    margin: 0;
    padding: 0;
  }
  .wrapper {
    display: grid;
    grid-template-columns: none;
  }
  .wrapper div span {
    font-size: 30px;
```

```css
}
.div-1 {
  background-color: aqua;
}
.div-2 {
  background-color: cornflowerblue;
}
.div-3 {
  background-color: limegreen;
}
.div-4 {
  background-color: darkorange;
}
.div-5 {
  background-color: hotpink;
}
.div-6 {
  background-color: mediumorchid;
}
.div-7 {
  background-color: springgreen;
}
.div-8 {
  background-color: lightsalmon;
```

```html
    }
    .div-9 {
      background-color: darkturquoise;
    }
</style>
<div class="wrapper">
  <div class="div-1">
    <span>1</span>
    <p>
      Lorem ipsum dolor sit amet
consectetur adipisicing elit. Aliquam
nostrum
      iure harum corrupti.
    </p>
  </div>
  <div class="div-2">
    <span>2</span>
    <p>
      Lorem ipsum dolor sit amet
consectetur adipisicing elit. Ullam
tempore
      repellendus?
    </p>
  </div>
```

```html
<div class="div-3">
  <span>3</span>
  <p>
    Lorem ipsum dolor sit amet
consectetur adipisicing elit. Distinctio
    consequatur?
  </p>
</div>
<div class="div-4">
  <span>4</span>
  <p>
    Lorem, ipsum dolor sit amet
consectetur adipisicing elit. Vero
consectetur
    pariatur explicabo culpa itaque
qui nostrum asperiores voluptatum alias?
  </p>
</div>
<div class="div-5">
  <span>5</span>
  <p>
    Lorem, ipsum dolor sit amet
consectetur adipisicing elit. Vero
consectetur
```

```html
      pariatur explicabo culpa itaque
qui nostrum asperiores voluptatum alias?
    </p>
  </div>
  <div class="div-6">
    <span>6</span>
    <p>Iusto excepturi adipisci
praesentium accusantium eius quis!</p>
  </div>
  <div class="div-7">
    <span>7</span>
    <p>
      Lorem, ipsum dolor sit amet
consectetur adipisicing elit. Vero
consectetur
      pariatur explicabo culpa itaque
qui nostrum asperiores voluptatum alias?
    </p>
  </div>
  <div class="div-8">
    <span>8</span>
    <p>
```

```
      Lorem, ipsum dolor sit amet
consectetur adipisicing elit. Vero
consectetur
      pariatur explicabo culpa itaque
qui nostrum asperiores voluptatum alias?
    </p>
  </div>
  <div class="div-9">
    <span>9</span>
    <p>
      Lorem, ipsum dolor sit amet
consectetur adipisicing elit. Vero
consectetur
      pariatur explicabo culpa itaque
qui nostrum asperiores voluptatum alias?
    </p>
  </div>
</div>
```

auto

The size of the columns depends on the size of the container and the size of the content of the articles in the column

```css
.wrapper {
  display: grid;
  grid-template-columns: auto;
}
```

max-content

Sets the size of each column to depend on the largest item in the column

```css
.wrapper {
  display: grid;
  grid-template-columns: max-content;
}
```

min-content

Sets the size of each column to depend on the smallest
item in the column

```css
.wrapper {
  display: grid;
  grid-template-columns: min-content;
}
```

length

Sets the size of the columns, by using a legal length value.

Set fixed width to the second column, 300px;

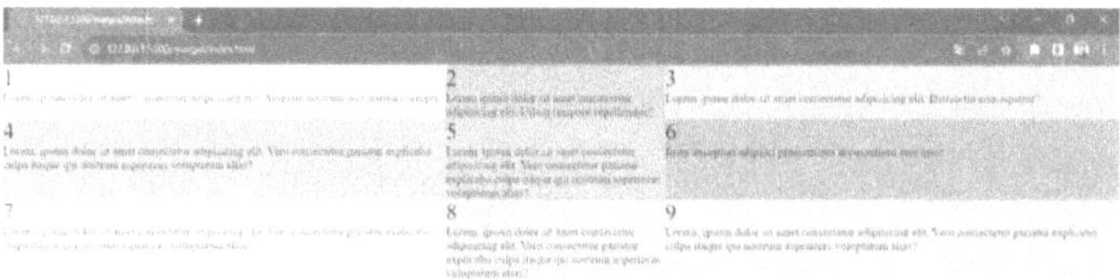

```css
.wrapper {
  display: grid;
  grid-template-columns: auto 300px auto;
}
```

%

Set the third column to be 50% of the container width:

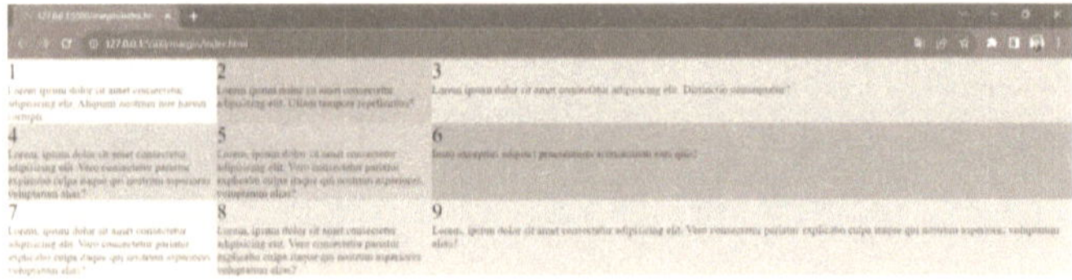

```
.wrapper {
  display: grid;
  grid-template-columns: auto auto 60%;
}
```

fr

The `fr` unit represents a fraction of the available space in the grid container.

Set the the third column to be 3 times larger than the second column, while giving the first column fixed 500px:

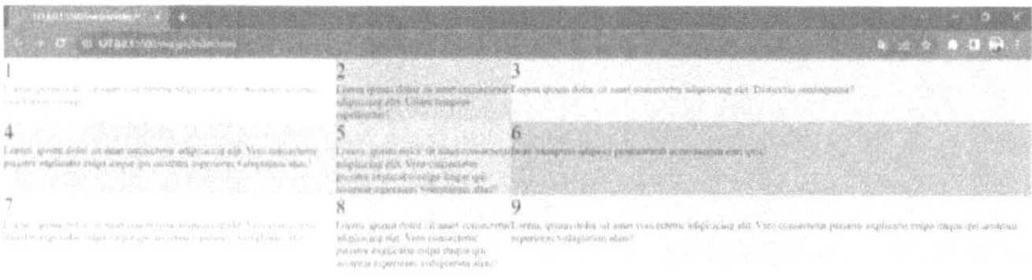

```css
.wrapper {
  display: grid;
  grid-template-columns: 500px 1fr 3fr;
}
```

minmax()

The CSS function minmax() defines a size range that is greater than or equal to min and less than or equal to max.

Set the second column has minimum 500px and maximum 2fr;

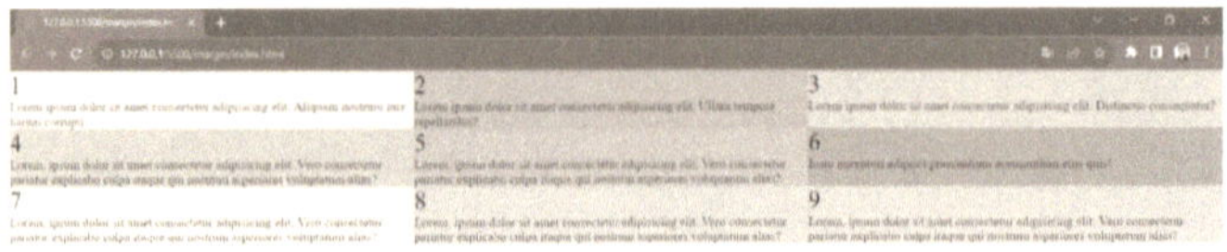

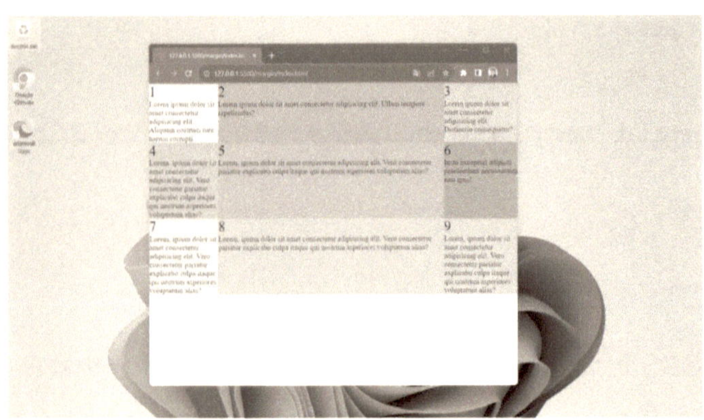

```css
.wrapper {
    display: grid;
    grid-template-columns: auto
minmax(500px, 2fr) auto;
}
```

repeat()

The CSS function repeat() represents a repeating fragment of the track list and makes it possible to write a large number of columns or rows that have a recurring pattern in a more compact form.

I want to have five columns and four of them will have the same width

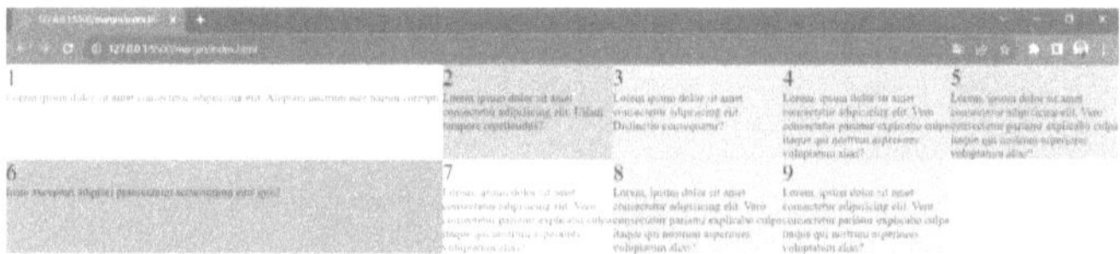

```
.wrapper {
    display: grid;
    grid-template-columns: auto 1fr 1fr 1fr 1fr;
}
```

You can use the repeat() function for such scenarios as follows

```
.wrapper {
  display: grid;
  grid-template-columns: auto repeat(4,
1fr);
  }
```

auto, repeat() and length

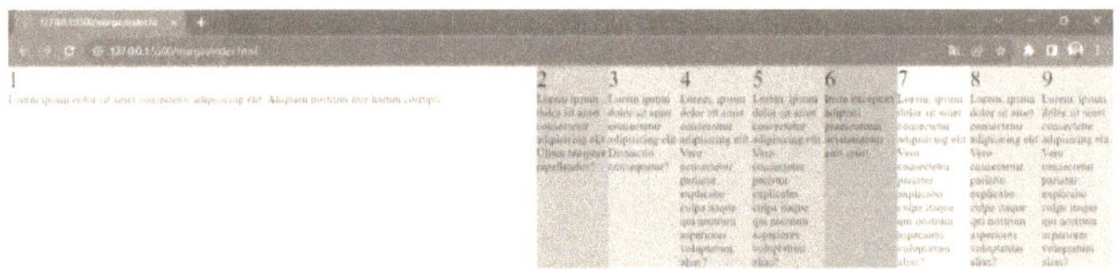

```
.wrapper {
  display: grid;
  grid-template-columns: auto repeat(8,
100px);
  }
```

grid-template-rows

The grid-template-rows property defines the number (and height) of rows in a grid layout.

The values are a space-separated list in which each value specifies the height of the respective row.

Values

- none
- auto
- max-content
- min-content
- length

none

No size is set. Rows are created if needed

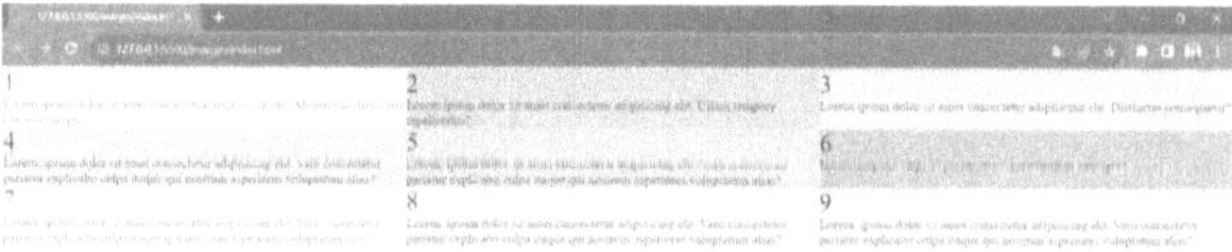

```
.wrapper {
```

```css
    display: grid;
    grid-template-columns: auto auto
auto;
    border: 3px dashed orangered;
    grid-template-rows: none;

  }
```

auto

The size of the rows is determined by the size of the
container, and on the size of the content of the items in
the row

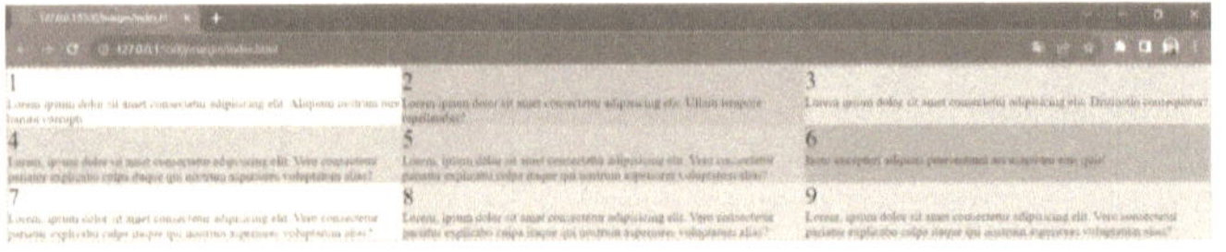

```css
  .wrapper {
    display: grid;
    grid-template-columns: auto auto
auto;
```

```css
  border: 3px dashed orangered;
  grid-template-rows: auto;
}
```

max-content

Sets the size of each row to depend on the largest item in the row

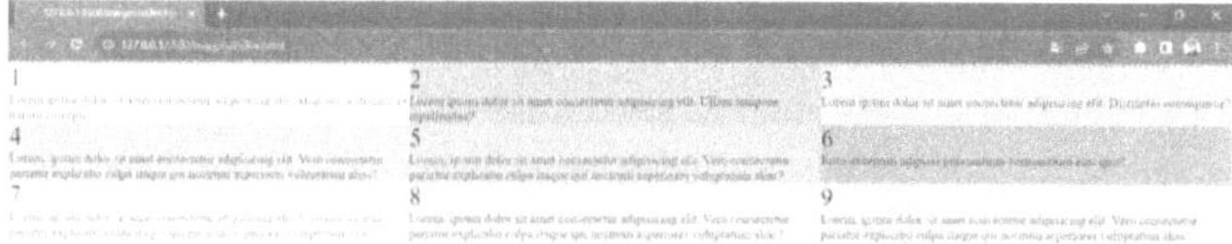

```css
.wrapper {
  display: grid;
  grid-template-columns: auto auto auto;
  border: 3px dashed orangered;
  grid-template-rows: max-content;
}
```

min-content

Sets the size of each row to depend on the smallest item in the row.

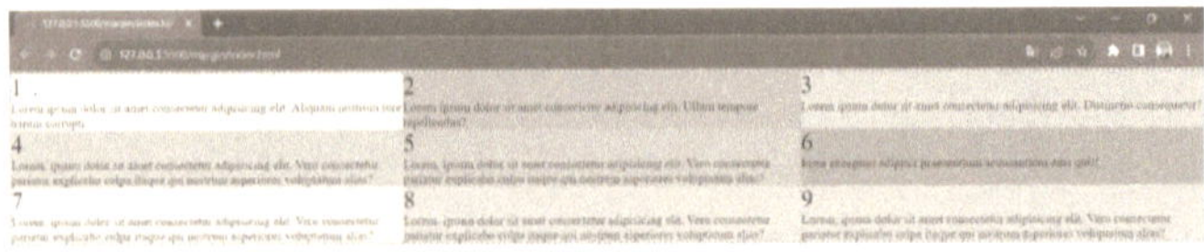

```
.wrapper {
  display: grid;
  grid-template-columns: auto auto auto;
  border: 3px dashed orangered;
  grid-template-rows: min-content;
}
```

length

Sets the size of the rows, by using a legal length value. Now we define four rows for the grid, each with a height of 150px:

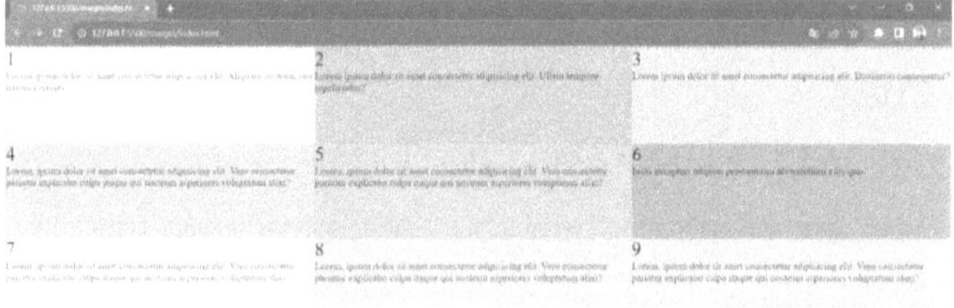

```
.wrapper {
  display: grid;
  border: 3px dashed orangered;
  grid-template-columns: auto auto
auto;
  grid-template-rows: repeat(4, 150px);
}
```

So far we have worked with the grid container and the grid tracks, now we want to talk about the grid elements. By this I mean the elements that are placed within the grid container.

Grid items can occupy one or more grid cells, spanning across multiple rows and columns.

Use the grid-column and grid-row properties to position and span the elements within the grid.

Grid lines

First you need to know about grid lines.

Grid lines are created when you define tracks in the CSS Grid Layout.

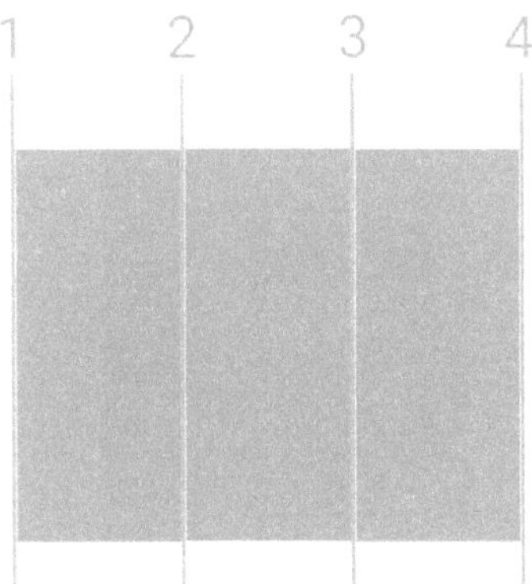

Here are the grid lines for a 3-column layout.

The same applies to the rows.

We use grid lines to determine the start and end for each grid element.

grid-column

The grid-column property defines the size and position of a grid element in a grid layout and is a short form for the grid-column-start and grid-column-end properties.

Values

- <grid-column-start> / <grid-column-end>

Values for grid-column-start and grid-column-end

- auto
- span n
- column-line

auto

Default value. The item will be placed following the flow

span n

Specifies the number of columns the item will span

column-line

Specifies in which column the display of the element should begin or end

grid-row

The grid-row property defines the size and position of a grid element in a grid layout and is a short form for the grid-row-start and grid-row-end properties

Values

- <grid-row-start> / <grid-row-end>

Values for grid-row-start and grid-row-end

- auto
- span n
- column-line

auto

Default value. The item will be placed following the flow

span n

Specifies the number of rows the item will span

row-line

Specifies in which row the display of the element should begin or end

auto

```css
.div-1 {
  background-color: aqua;
  grid-column: auto;
  grid-row: auto;
}
```

span n

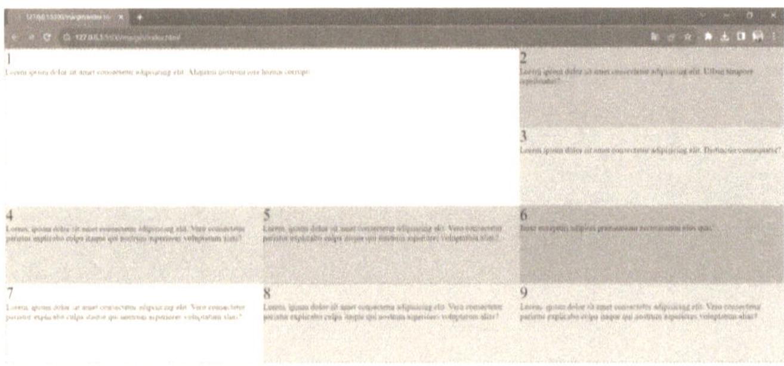

```css
.div-1 {
  background-color: aqua;
  grid-column: 1 / span 2;
  grid-row: 1 / span 2;
}
```

column-line and row-line

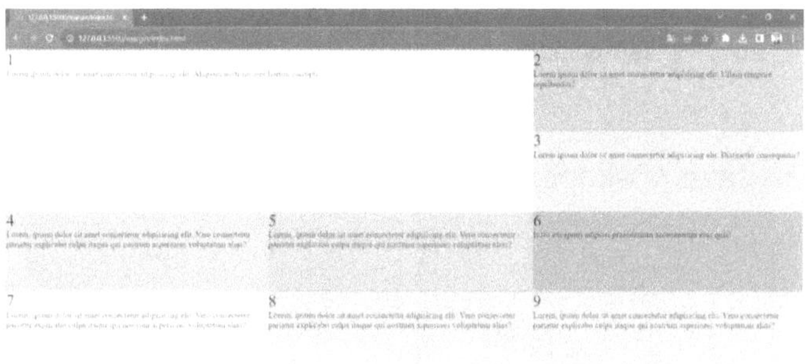

```
.div-1 {
   background-color: aqua;
   grid-column: 1 / 3;
   grid-row: 1 / 3;
}
```

For the column, I specify that it begins in line 1 and ends in line 3.

I do the same for the row, I set it so that it starts in line 1 and ends in line 3.

So you can write the code like this and it will give the same result

```
.div-1 {
    background-color: aqua;
    grid-column-start: 1;
```

```css
    grid-column-end: 3;
    grid-row-start: 1;
    grid-row-end: 3;
}
```

For the sake of simplicity, I use the shorthand property.

```css
.div-1 {
    background-color: aqua;
    grid-column: 1 / 3;
    grid-row: 1 / 3;
}
```

negative lines

If a negative integer is specified, it is counted backwards instead, starting with the end edge of the explicit grid. For example, I can span all columns by setting start to 1 and end to -1, as follows

```css
.div-1 {
  background-color: aqua;
  grid-column: 1 / -1;
  grid-row: 1 / 3;
}
```

backwards

Negatives are counted backwards, starting with the end edge of the explicit grid.

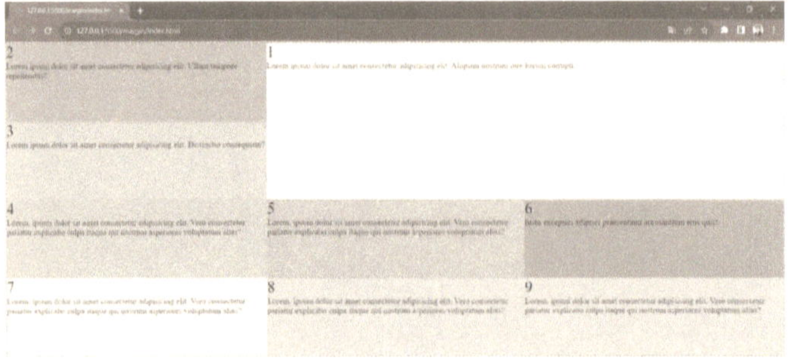

```
.div-1 {
  background-color: aqua;
  grid-column: -1 / -3;
  grid-row: 1 / 3;
}
```

grid-template-areas

The grid-template-areas property defines areas within the grid layout.

Each area is defined by apostrophes. Use a dot character to refer to a grid element without a name.

Values

- none
- areas

none

none

Default value. No named grid areas

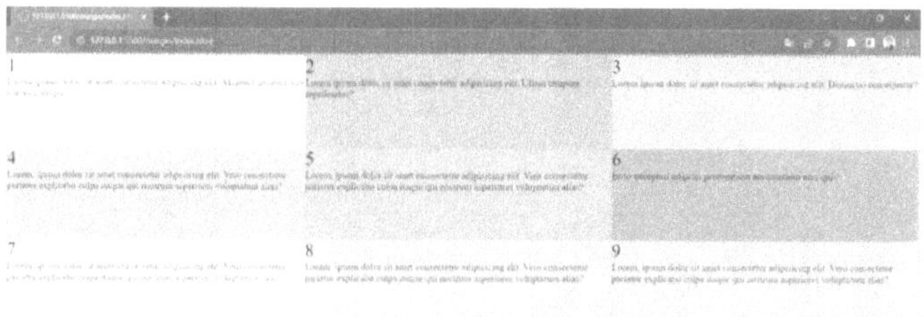

```
.wrapper {
    display: grid;
    border: 3px dashed orangered;
    grid-template-columns: auto auto
auto;
    grid-template-rows: repeat(4,
150px);
    grid-template-areas: none;
  }
```

areas

A sequence that specifies how each columns and row
should display

Each area is defined by apostrophes.

Use a dot character to refer to a grid element without a name.

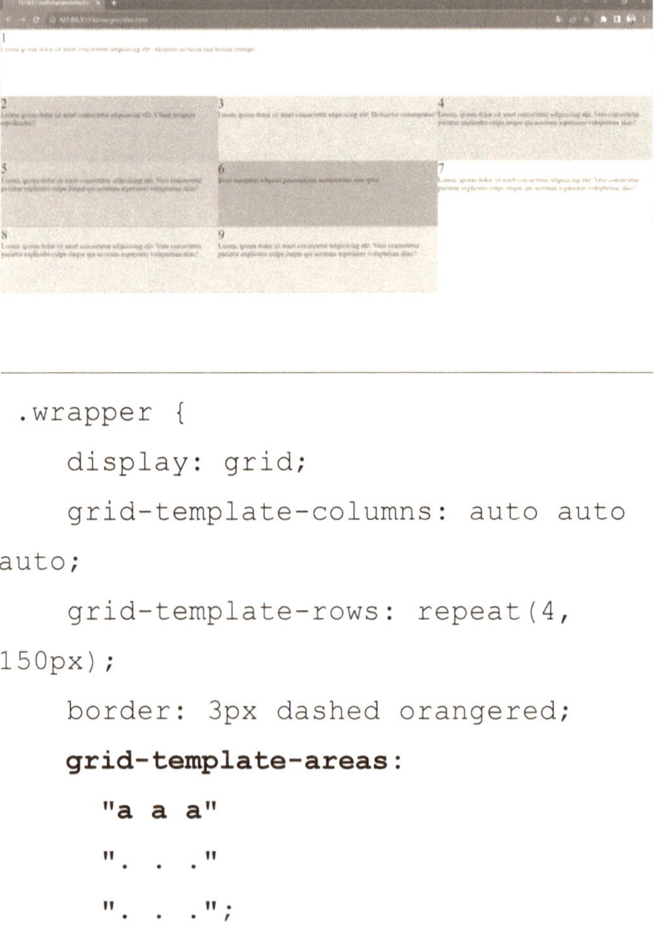

```css
.wrapper {
    display: grid;
    grid-template-columns: auto auto auto;
    grid-template-rows: repeat(4, 150px);
    border: 3px dashed orangered;
    grid-template-areas:
        "a a a"
        ". . ."
        ". . .";
}
```

For the children elements, I want the .div-1 element to display in the "a" area.

```css
.div-1 {
  background-color: aqua;
  grid-area: a;
}
```

Here's the complete code:

```css
<style>
  * {
    margin: 0;
    padding: 0;
  }
  .wrapper {
    display: grid;
    grid-template-columns: auto auto auto;
    grid-template-rows: repeat(4, 150px);
    border: 3px dashed orangered;
    grid-template-areas:
      "a a a"
      "b c c"
      "b c c";
```

```css
}
.wrapper div span {
  font-size: 30px;
}
.div-1 {
  background-color: aqua;
  grid-area: a;
}
.div-2 {
  background-color: cornflowerblue;
}
.div-3 {
  background-color: limegreen;
}
.div-4 {
  background-color: darkorange;
}
.div-5 {
  background-color: hotpink;
}
.div-6 {
  background-color: mediumorchid;
}
.div-7 {
```

```html
      background-color: springgreen;
    }
    .div-8 {
      background-color: lightsalmon;
    }
    .div-9 {
      background-color: darkturquoise;
    }
</style>
<div class="wrapper">
  <div class="div-1">
    <span>1</span>
    <p>
      Lorem ipsum dolor sit amet
consectetur adipisicing elit. Aliquam
nostrum
      iure harum corrupti.
    </p>
  </div>
  <div class="div-2">
    <span>2</span>
    <p>
```

```html
      Lorem ipsum dolor sit amet
consectetur adipisicing elit. Ullam
tempore
      repellendus?
    </p>
  </div>
  <div class="div-3">
    <span>3</span>
    <p>
      Lorem ipsum dolor sit amet
consectetur adipisicing elit. Distinctio
      consequatur?
    </p>
  </div>
  <div class="div-4">
    <span>4</span>
    <p>
      Lorem, ipsum dolor sit amet
consectetur adipisicing elit. Vero
consectetur
      pariatur explicabo culpa itaque
qui nostrum asperiores voluptatum alias?
    </p>
  </div>
```

```
<div class="div-5">
  <span>5</span>
  <p>
    Lorem, ipsum dolor sit amet
consectetur adipisicing elit. Vero
consectetur
    pariatur explicabo culpa itaque
qui nostrum asperiores voluptatum alias?
  </p>
</div>
<div class="div-6">
  <span>6</span>
  <p>Iusto excepturi adipisci
praesentium accusantium eius quis!</p>
</div>
<div class="div-7">
  <span>7</span>
  <p>
    Lorem, ipsum dolor sit amet
consectetur adipisicing elit. Vero
consectetur
    pariatur explicabo culpa itaque
qui nostrum asperiores voluptatum alias?
  </p>
```

```html
    </div>
    <div class="div-8">
      <span>8</span>
      <p>
        Lorem, ipsum dolor sit amet
consectetur adipisicing elit. Vero
consectetur
        pariatur explicabo culpa itaque
qui nostrum asperiores voluptatum alias?
      </p>
    </div>
    <div class="div-9">
      <span>9</span>
      <p>
        Lorem, ipsum dolor sit amet
consectetur adipisicing elit. Vero
consectetur
        pariatur explicabo culpa itaque
qui nostrum asperiores voluptatum alias?
      </p>
    </div>
</div>
```

You can give it meaningful names like "head", "nav", "main" … etc.

```
.wrapper {
  display: grid;
  grid-template-columns: auto auto auto;
  grid-template-rows: repeat(4, 150px);
  border: 3px dashed orangered;
  grid-template-areas:
    "head head head"
    "nav main main"
    "nav main main";
}
```

gap

grid-gap is obsolete and is replaced by **gap**

The gap property defines the size of the gap between the rows and columns in a grid layout, and is a shorthand property for the following properties: row-gap and column-gap

Values

- <row-gap> <column-gap>

gap: 20px;

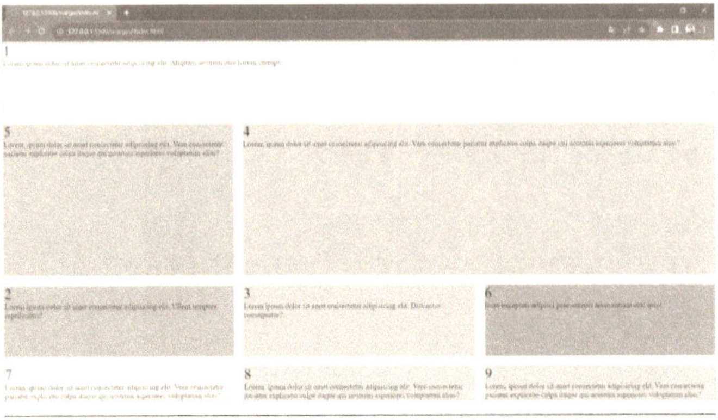

```css
.wrapper {
  display: grid;
  grid-template-columns: auto auto auto;
  grid-template-rows: repeat(4, 150px);
  border: 3px dashed orangered;
  grid-template-areas:
    "a a a"
    ". . ."
    ". . .";
  gap: 20px;
}
```

gap: 50px 10px;

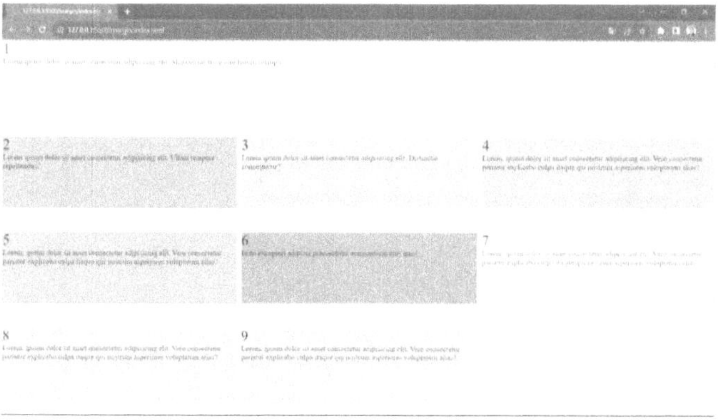

```css
.wrapper {
  display: grid;
  grid-template-columns: auto auto auto;
  grid-template-rows: repeat(4, 150px);
  border: 3px dashed orangered;
  grid-template areas:
    "a a a"
    ". . ."
    ". . .";
  gap: 50px 10px;
}
```

column-gap: 20px;

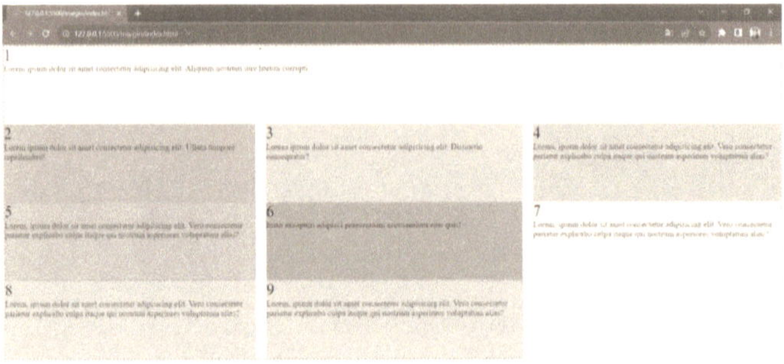

```css
.wrapper {
    display: grid;
    grid-template-columns: auto auto
auto;
    grid-template-rows: repeat(4,
150px);
    border: 3px dashed orangered;
    grid-template-areas:
        "a a a"
        ". . ."
        ". . .";
    column-gap: 20px;
}
```

row-gap: 20px;

```css
.wrapper {
  display: grid;
  grid-template-columns: auto auto auto;
  grid-template-rows: repeat(4, 150px);
  border: 3px dashed orangered;
  grid-template-areas:
    "a a a"
    ". . ."
    ". . .";
  row-gap: 20px;
}
```

Alignment and Justification

CSS Grid Layout is a two-dimensional layout method that makes it possible to arrange content in rows and columns. Therefore, there are two axes in each grid. The block or column axis and the inline or row axis.

Inline Axis

The inline axis is the axis that corresponds to the direction in which the words in a sentence would run in the spelling used. In a horizontal language such as English or Arabic, the inline direction is therefore horizontal. In a vertical writing mode, the inline axis is vertical.

To align things on the inline axis, use the properties that start with justify-, justify-content, justify-items and justify-self.

Block axis

The block axis crosses the inline axis in the direction in which the blocks are displayed on the page — for example, paragraphs are displayed vertically one below the other in English. This is therefore the block dimension.

To align things to the block axis, use the properties that start with align-, align-content, align-items and align-self.

justify-content

The CSS property justify-content determines how the browser distributes the space between and around content elements along the inline axis of a grid container.

Values

- start or flex-start
- end or flex-end
- center
- space-between
- space-around
- space-evenly

start or flex-start

Default value. Items are positioned at the beginning of the container

`flex-start` is specific to flex layout, but if you use it with grid layout, it will be treated as `start`.

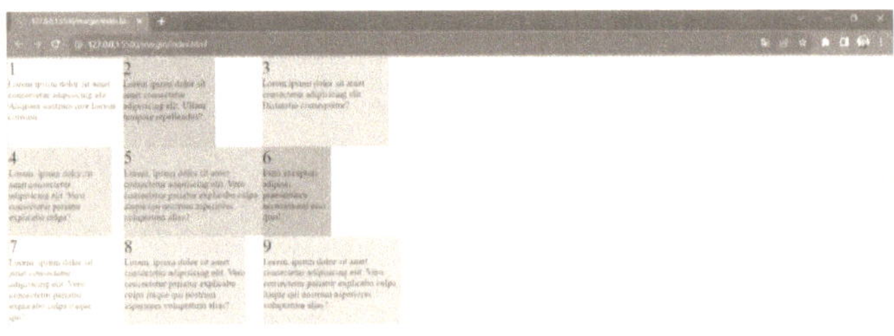

```
<style>
  * {
    margin: 0;
```

```css
    padding: 0;
  }
  .wrapper {
    display: grid;
    grid-template-columns: auto auto
auto;
    grid-template-rows: repeat(4,
150px);
    border: 3px dashed orangered;
    justify-content: start;
  }
  .wrapper div span {
    font-size: 30px;
  }
  .div-1 {
    background-color: aqua;
    width: 200px;
  }
  .div-2 {
    background-color: cornflowerblue;
    width: 160px;
  }
  .div-3 {
    background-color: limegreen;
```

```css
    width: 220px;
}
.div-4 {
  background-color: darkorange;
  width: 180px;
}
.div-5 {
  background-color: hotpink;
  width: 240px;
}
.div-6 {
  background-color: mediumorchid;
  width: 120px;
}
.div-7 {
  background-color: springgreen;
  width: 170px;
}
.div-8 {
  background-color: lightsalmon;
  width: 210px;
}
.div-9 {
  background-color: darkturquoise;
```

```
      width: 240px;
    }
</style>
<div class="wrapper">
  <div class="div-1">
    <span>1</span>
    <p>
      Lorem ipsum dolor sit amet
consectetur adipisicing elit. Aliquam
nostrum
      iure harum corrupti.
    </p>
  </div>
  <div class="div-2">
    <span>2</span>
    <p>
      Lorem ipsum dolor sit amet
consectetur adipisicing elit. Ullam
tempore
      repellendus?
    </p>
  </div>
  <div class="div-3">
    <span>3</span>
```

```
      <p>
        Lorem ipsum dolor sit amet
  consectetur adipisicing elit. Distinctio
        consequatur?
      </p>
    </div>
    <div class="div-4">
      <span>4</span>
      <p>
        Lorem, ipsum dolor sit amet
  consectetur adipisicing elit. Vero
  consectetur
        pariatur explicabo culpa?
      </p>
    </div>
    <div class="div-5">
      <span>5</span>
      <p>
        Lorem, ipsum dolor sit amet
  consectetur adipisicing elit. Vero
  consectetur
        pariatur explicabo culpa itaque
  qui nostrum asperiores voluptatum alias?
      </p>
```

```html
    </div>
    <div class="div-6">
      <span>6</span>
      <p>Iusto excepturi adipisci
praesentium accusantium eius quis!</p>
    </div>
    <div class="div-7">
      <span>7</span>
      <p>
        Lorem, ipsum dolor sit amet
consectetur adipisicing elit. Vero
consectetur
        pariatur explicabo culpa itaque
qui?
      </p>
    </div>
    <div class="div-8">
      <span>8</span>
      <p>
        Lorem, ipsum dolor sit amet
consectetur adipisicing elit. Vero
consectetur
        pariatur explicabo culpa itaque
qui nostrum asperiores voluptatum alias?
```

```
    </p>
  </div>
  <div class="div-9">
    <span>9</span>
    <p>
      Lorem, ipsum dolor sit amet
consectetur adipisicing elit. Vero
consectetur
      pariatur explicabo culpa itaque
qui nostrum asperiores voluptatum alias?
    </p>
  </div>
</div>
```

end or flex-end

Items are positioned at the end of the container
`flex-end` is specific to flex layout, but if you use it with
grid layout, it will be treated as `end`.

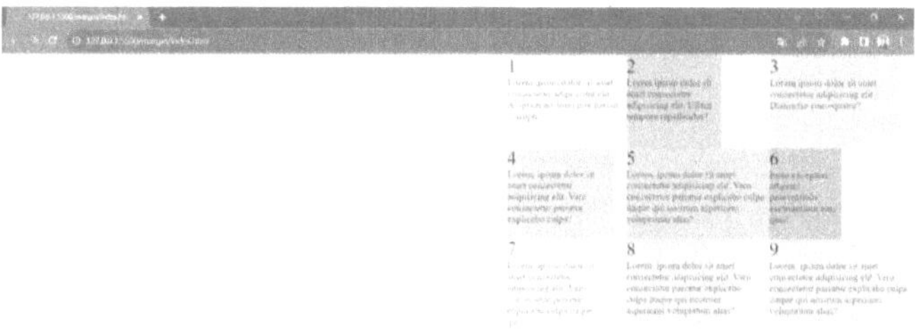

```
.wrapper {
   display: grid;
   grid-template-columns: auto auto auto;
   grid-template-rows: repeat(4, 150px);
   border: 3px dashed orangered;
   justify-content: end;
}
```

center

Items are positioned in the center of the container

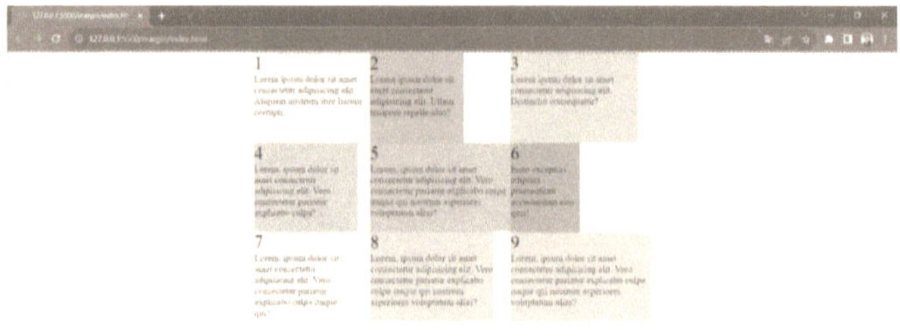

```css
.wrapper {
  display: grid;
  grid-template-columns: auto auto auto;
  grid-template-rows: repeat(4, 150px);
  border: 3px dashed orangered;
  justify-content: center;
}
```

space-between

Items will have space between them

```css
.wrapper {
  display: grid;
  grid-template-columns: auto auto auto;
  grid-template-rows: repeat(4, 150px);
  border: 3px dashed orangered;
  justify-content: space-between;
}
```

space-around

Items will have space before, between, and after them

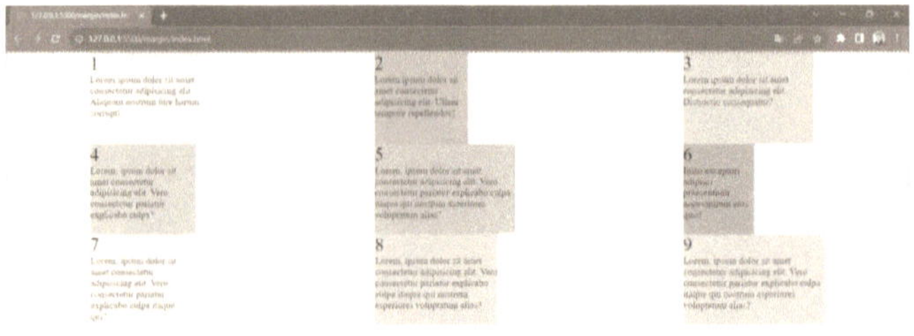

```
.wrapper {
    display: grid;
    grid-template-columns: auto auto
auto;
    grid-template-rows: repeat(4,
150px);
    border: 3px dashed orangered;
    justify-content: space-around;
}
```

space-evenly

Items will have equal space around them

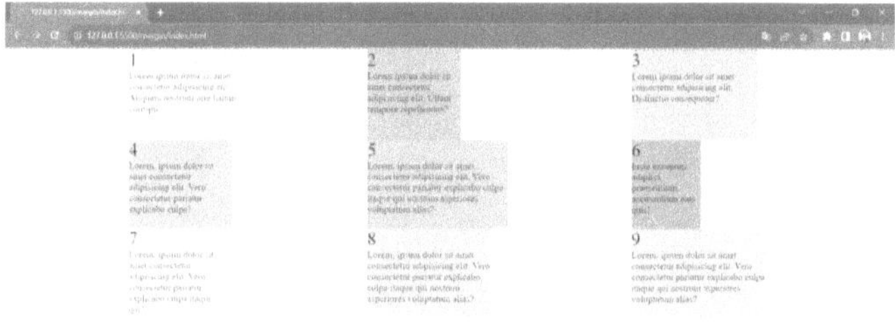

```css
.wrapper {
  display: grid;
  grid-template-columns: auto auto auto;
  grid-template-rows: repeat(4, 150px);
  border: 3px dashed orangered;
  justify-content: space-evenly;
}
```

justify-items

The CSS property justify-items sets the default alignment for all elements of the box and thus gives them a default alignment along the corresponding axis.

Values

- normal or stretch
- start
- left
- center
- end
- right
- baseline

normal or stretch

Stretches to fill the grid cell if inline-size (width) is not set.

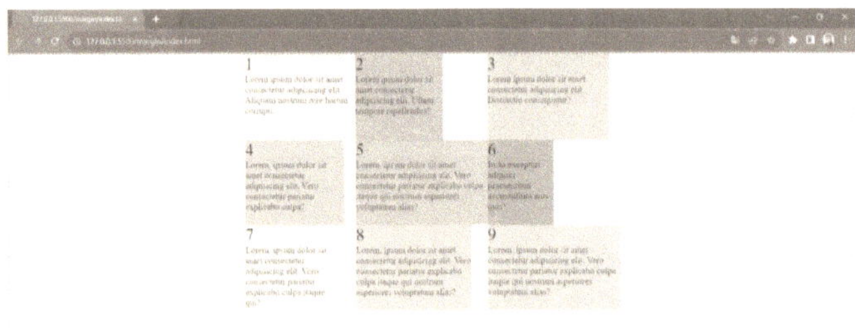

```
.wrapper {
  display: grid;
  grid-template-columns: auto auto auto;
```

```css
    grid-template-rows: repeat(4,
150px);
    border: 3px dashed orangered;
    justify-content: center;
    justify-items: normal;
}
```

start

Align items at the start in the inline direction

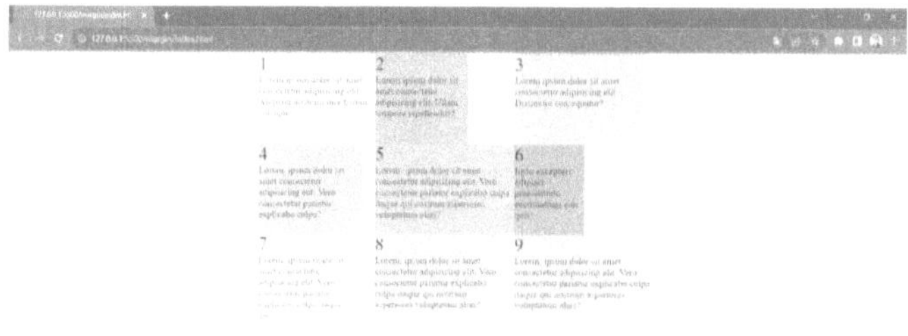

```css
  .wrapper {
    display: grid;
    grid-template-columns: auto auto
auto;
    grid-template-rows: repeat(4,
150px);
```

```css
    border: 3px dashed orangered;
    justify-content: center;
    justify-items: start;
}
```

end

Align items to the left

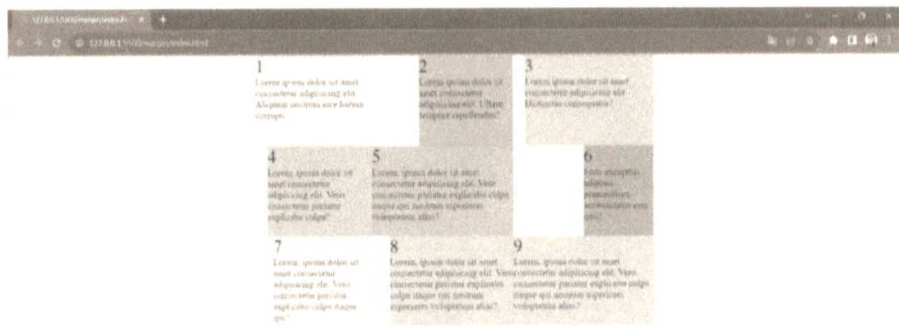

```css
.wrapper {
    display: grid;
    grid-template-columns: auto auto
auto;
    grid-template-rows: repeat(4,
150px);
    border: 3px dashed orangered;
    justify-content: center;
```

```css
    justify-items: end;
}
```

center

Align items to the center

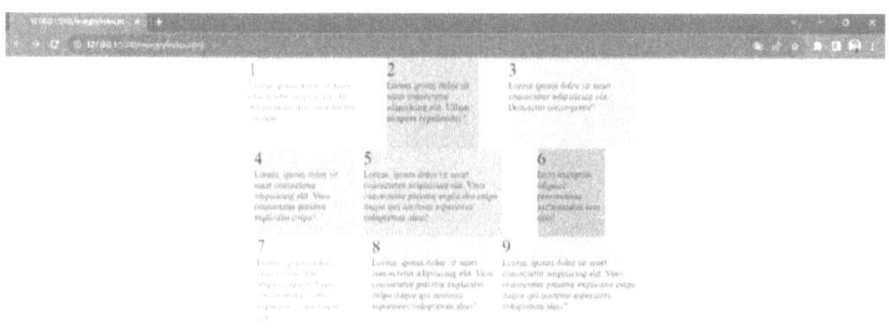

```css
.wrapper {
    display: grid;
    grid-template-columns: auto auto auto;
    grid-template-rows: repeat(4, 150px);
    border: 3px dashed orangered;
    justify-content: center;
    justify-items: center;
}
```

justify-self

The CSS property justify-self defines how an element should be justified. It overrides the justify-items of the container.

justify-self is set per child, not on the grid container.

Values

- normal
- stretch
- start
- left
- center
- end
- right
- baseline

I will give you an example and you can try them all

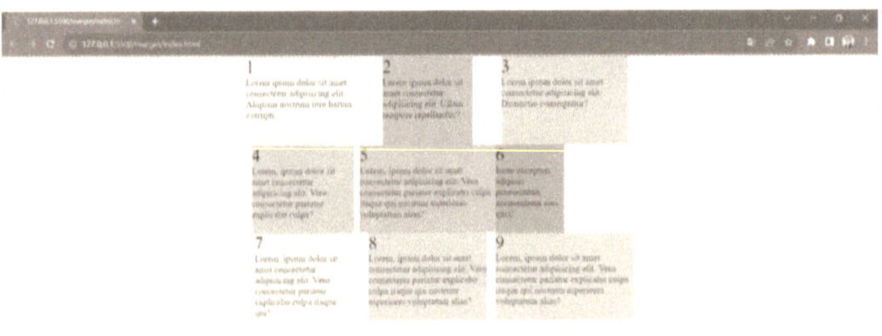

```css
.div-6 {
  background-color: mediumorchid;
  width: 120px;
  justify-self: start;
}
```

align-content

The CSS property align-content defines the distribution
of the space between and around content elements
along the block axis of a grid.

- The `justify-content` and `align-content`
  properties align **the grid**.
- The `justify-self`, `justify-items`,
  `align-self` and `align-items` properties, on
  the other hand, align **the elements of the grid**.

Values

- stretch
- center
- start or flex-start
- end or flex-end
- space-between
- space-around
- space-evenly

I will explain some of the values and you can try them all out.

center

Lines are packed toward the center of the flex container

```
.wrapper {
  display: grid;
  width: 90%;
  height: 90%;
  grid-template-columns: auto auto auto;
  grid-template-rows: repeat(4, 150px);
  border: 3px dashed orangered;
```

```
    justify-content: start;
    align-content: center;
  }
```

You can see that the grid - delimited by dotted lines - is centered within the grid container. This is the effect of align-content: center;

However, not every item is centered in its row, and we can achieve that with align-items: center;, which we'll see in a moment.

start

The objects are packed together flush at the starting edge of the alignment container in the transverse axis.

```
  .wrapper {
    display: grid;
```

```css
    width: 90%;
    height: 90%;
    grid-template-columns: auto auto
auto;
    grid-template-rows: repeat(4,
150px);
    border: 3px dashed orangered;
    justify-content: start;
    align-content: start;
  }
```

align-items

The CSS property align-items sets the value align-self to all direct children as a group. It controls the alignment of the elements on the block axis within their grid area.

Values

- normal or stretch
- center
- start
- end
- baseline

I will explain some of the values and you can try them all out.

start

Items are positioned at the beginning of their individual grid cells, in the block direction

```
.wrapper {
  display: grid;
  width: 90%;
  height: 90%;
  grid-template-columns: auto auto auto;
  grid-template-rows: repeat(4, 150px);
  border: 3px dashed orangered;
  justify-content: start;
```

```css
    align-content: center;
    align-items: start;
  }
```

In this example, you can see that the grid elements are aligned at the beginning, while the grid is centered in its container;

end

Items are positioned at the end of the their individual grid cells, in the block direction

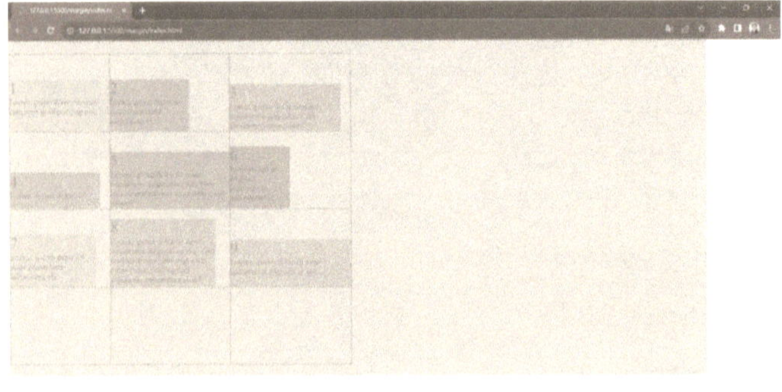

```css
  .wrapper {
    display: grid;
    width: 90%;
    height: 90%;
```

```css
    grid-template-columns: auto auto
auto;
    grid-template-rows: repeat(4,
150px);
    border: 3px dashed orangered;
    justify-content: start;
    align-content: center;
    align-items: end;
  }
```

center

Items are positioned at the center of the container

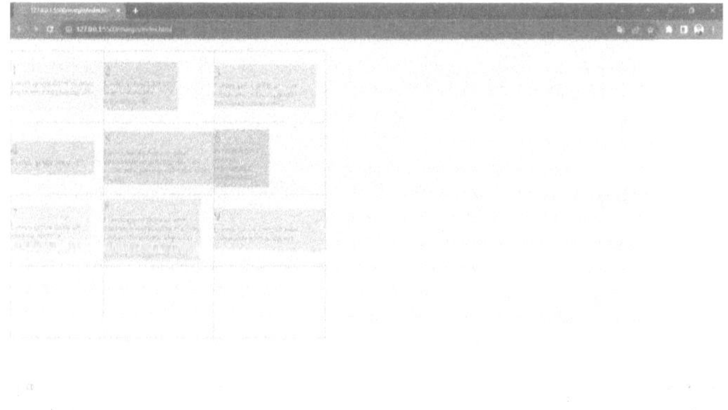

```css
  .wrapper {
    display: grid;
    width: 90%;
```

```css
    height: 90%;
    grid-template-columns: auto auto auto;
    grid-template-rows: repeat(4, 150px);
    border: 3px dashed orangered;
    justify-content: start;
    align-content: center;
    align-items: center;
  }
```

align-self

The CSS property align-self overrides the value align-items of the container.

Values

- stretch
- center
- start, flex-start or self-start
- end, flex-end or self-end
- baseline

start

The element is positioned at the beginning of the container

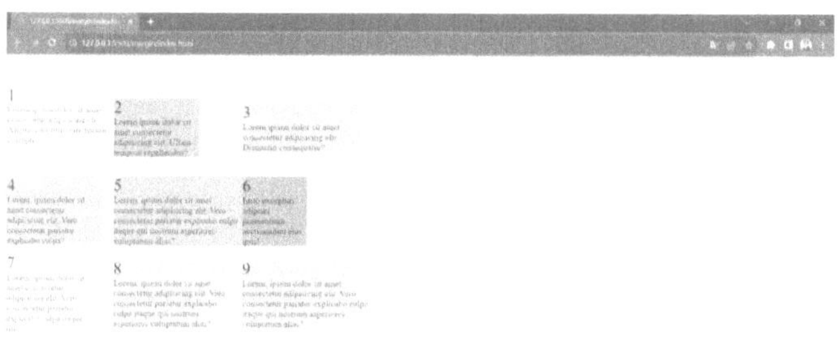

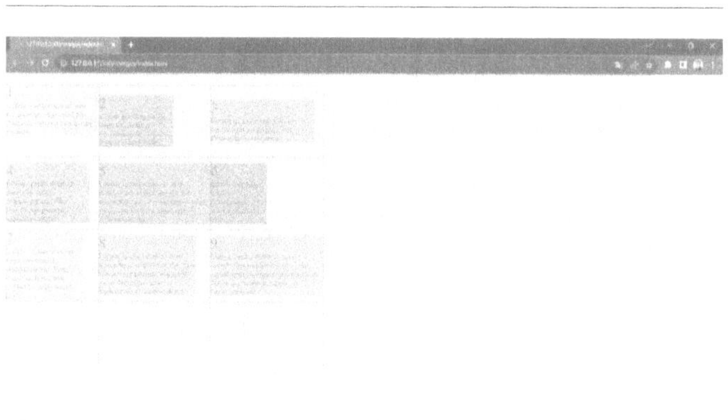

```css
.div-1 {
  background-color: aqua;
  width: 200px;
  align-self: start;
```

}

place-items

The CSS shorthand property "place-items" allows you to align items along the block and inline directions simultaneously. If the second value is not set, the first value is also used.

place-items: <align-items> <justify-items>

Values

- <align-items> <justify-items>

center

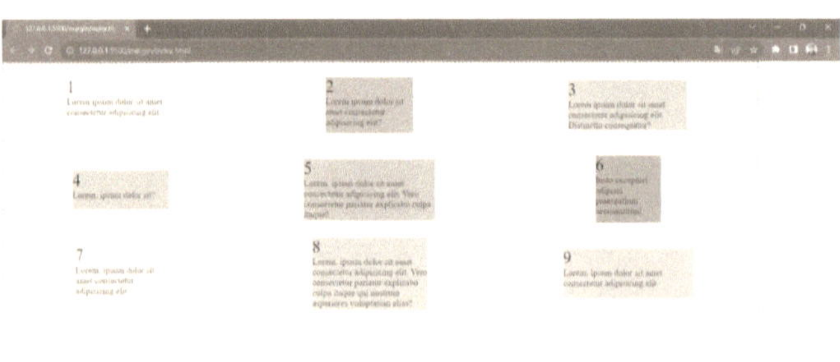

```
.wrapper {
  display: grid;
  width: 90%;
  height: 90%;
  grid-template-columns: auto auto
auto;
  grid-template-rows: repeat(4,
150px);
  border: 3px dashed orangered;
  place-items: center;
}
```

center end

Specify the end as the value for the inline axis

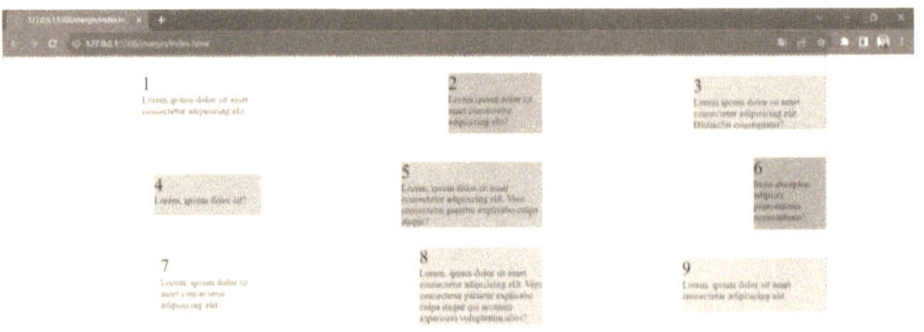

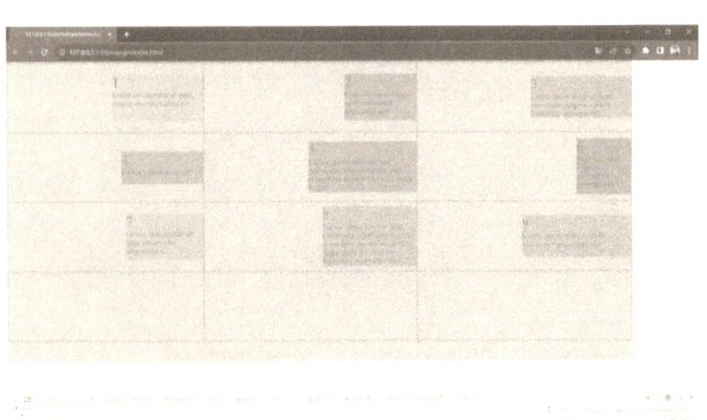

```css
.wrapper {
    display: grid;
    width: 90%;
    height: 90%;
    grid-template-columns: auto auto
auto;
    grid-template-rows: repeat(4,
150px);
```

```
    border: 3px dashed orangered;
    place-items: center end;
}
```

place-self

With the CSS shortcode property place-self, you can align a single item in both the block and inline directions at the same time. If the second value is not available, the first value is also used for it.

place-self: <align-self> <justify-self>

Values

- <align-self> <justify-self>

I will apply place-self to the .div-5 element to place it start center

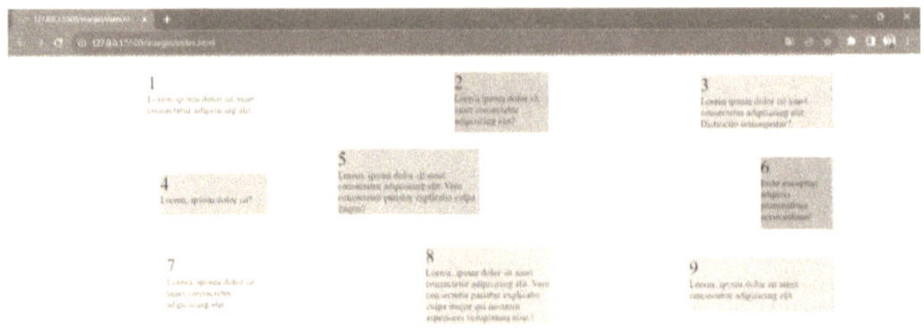

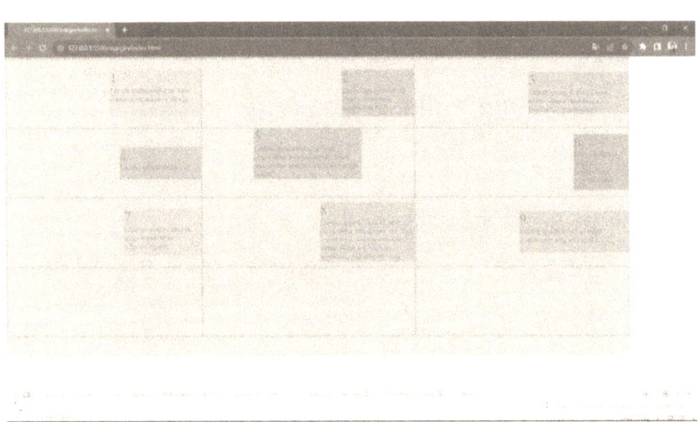

```css
.div-5 {
  background-color: hotpink;
  width: 240px;
  place-self: start center;
}
```

grid-auto-flow

The grid-auto-flow property controls how automatically placed elements are inserted into the grid.

Values

- row
- column
- dense
- row dense
- column dense

What if we add many div elements to our grid but don't specify in which grid area they should be placed?

This is where grid-auto-flow comes into play. By default, the elements are placed so that they fill the rows. But you can also change it so that it fills columns or gaps first.

row

Default value. Places items by filling each row

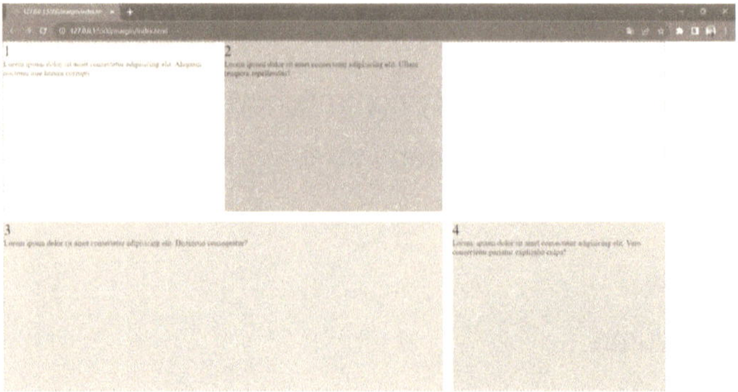

```
<style>
  * {
    margin: 0;
    padding: 0;
  }
  .wrapper {
    display: grid;
    width: 90%;
    height: 90%;
    grid-template-columns: auto auto auto;
    grid-template-rows: auto auto;
    border: 3px dashed orangered;
    gap: 20px;
    grid-auto-flow: row;
  }
```

```css
  .wrapper div span {
    font-size: 30px;
  }
  .div-1 {
    background-color: aqua;
  }
  .div-2 {
    background-color: cornflowerblue;
  }
  .div-3 {
    background-color: limegreen;
    grid-column: auto / span 2;
  }
  .div-4 {
    background-color: darkorange;
  }
</style>
<div class="wrapper">
  <div class="div-1">
    <span>1</span>
    <p>
      Lorem ipsum dolor sit amet
consectetur adipisicing elit. Aliquam
nostrum
```

```html
      iure harum corrupti.
    </p>
  </div>
  <div class="div-2">
    <span>2</span>
    <p>
      Lorem ipsum dolor sit amet
consectetur adipisicing elit. Ullam
tempore
        repellendus?
    </p>
  </div>
  <div class="div-3">
    <span>3</span>
    <p>
      Lorem ipsum dolor sit amet
consectetur adipisicing elit. Distinctio
        consequatur?
    </p>
  </div>
  <div class="div-4">
    <span>4</span>
    <p>
```

```
        Lorem, ipsum dolor sit amet
consectetur adipisicing elit. Vero
consectetur
        pariatur explicabo culpa?
    </p>
  </div>
</div>
```

row dense

If you set grid-auto-flow: row dense, all gaps are filled first as follows

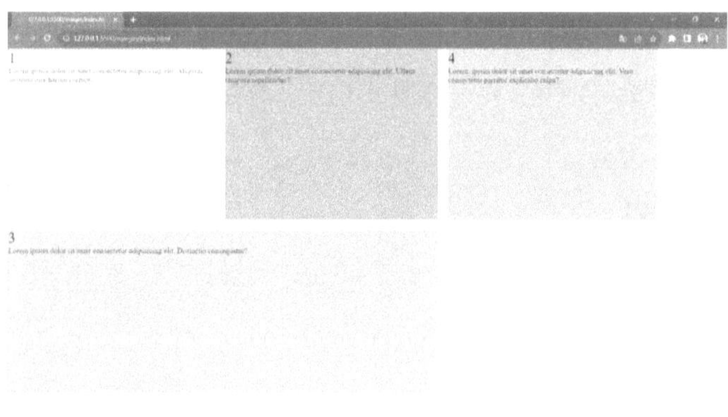

```
  .wrapper {
    display: grid;
    width: 90%;
    height: 90%;
```

```css
    grid-template-columns: auto auto
auto;
    grid-template-rows: auto auto;
    border: 3px dashed orangered;
    gap: 20px;
    grid-auto-flow: row dense;
  }
```

The same goes for grid-auto-flow: column and
grid-auto-flow: column dense;

grid-auto-rows

The grid-auto-rows CSS property specifies the size of
an implicitly-created grid row track or pattern of tracks.

Values

- auto
- row
- max-content
- min-content
- length

length

Sets the size of the rows, by using a legal length value.

For example, I set 140px for each newly created dynamic row:

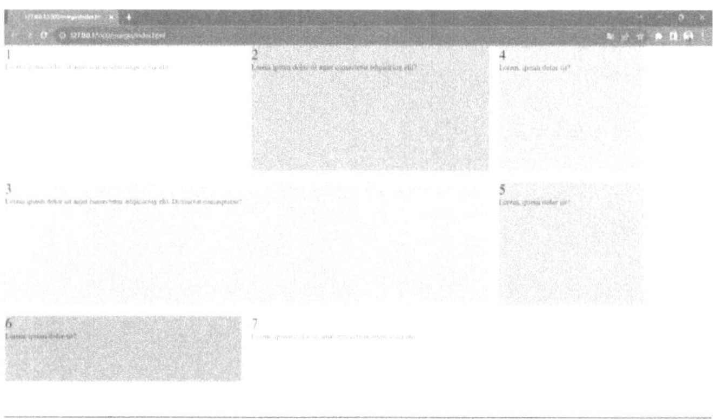

```
<style>
  * {
    margin: 0;
    padding: 0;
  }
  .wrapper {
    display: grid;
    width: 90%;
    height: 90%;
    grid-template-columns: auto auto auto;
    grid-template-rows: auto auto;
    border: 3px dashed orangered;
    gap: 20px;
```

```css
  grid-auto-flow: row dense;
  grid-auto-rows: 140px;
}
.wrapper div span {
  font-size: 30px;
}
.div-1 {
  background-color: aqua;
}
.div-2 {
  background-color: cornflowerblue;
}
.div-3 {
  background-color: limegreen;
  grid-column: auto / span 2;
}
.div-4 {
  background-color: darkorange;
}
.div-5 {
  background-color: hotpink;
}
.div-6 {
  background-color: mediumorchid;
```

```html
      }
      .div-7 {
        background-color: springgreen;
      }
</style>
<div class="wrapper">
  <div class="div-1">
    <span>1</span>
    <p>
      Lorem ipsum dolor sit amet
consectetur adipisicing elit. Aliquam
nostrum
      iure harum corrupti.
    </p>
  </div>
  <div class="div-2">
    <span>2</span>
    <p>
      Lorem ipsum dolor sit amet
consectetur adipisicing elit. Ullam
tempore
      repellendus?
    </p>
  </div>
```

```
<div class="div-3">
  <span>3</span>
  <p>
    Lorem ipsum dolor sit amet
consectetur adipisicing elit. Distinctio
    consequatur?
  </p>
</div>
<div class="div-4">
  <span>4</span>
  <p>
    Lorem, ipsum dolor sit amet
consectetur adipisicing elit. Vero
consectetur
    pariatur explicabo culpa?
  </p>
</div>
<div class="div-5">
  <span>5</span>
  <p>Lorem, ipsum dolor sit?</p>
</div>
<div class="div-6">
  <span>6</span>
  <p>Lorem, ipsum dolor sit?</p>
```

```html
    </div>
    <div class="div-7">
      <span>7</span>
      <p>Lorem, ipsum dolor sit amet
consectetur adipisicing elit.</p>
    </div>
</div>
```

grid-auto-columns

The CSS property grid-auto-columns defines the size of
the implicitly created grid columns.

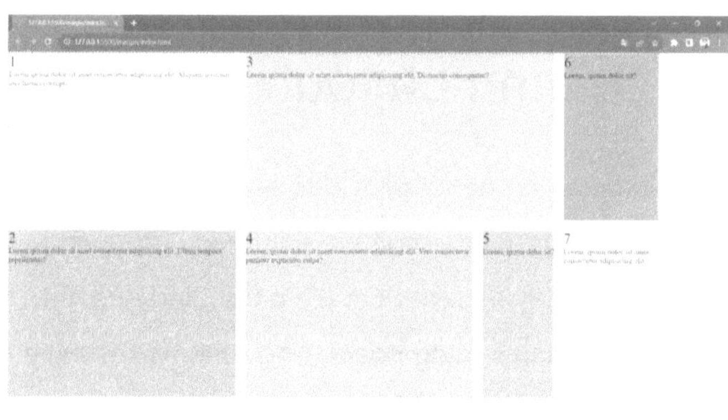

```css
.wrapper {
    display: grid;
    width: 90%;
    height: 90%;
```

```css
    grid-template-columns: auto auto auto;
    grid-template-rows: auto auto;
    border: 3px dashed orangered;
    gap: 20px;
    grid-auto-rows: 140px;
    grid-auto-flow: column dense;
    grid-auto-columns: 200px;
}
```

This concludes the section on the grid layout. Have fun coding!

Multi-column Layout

CSS3 Multi-column Layout provides an effective way to organize text content into multiple columns, improving readability and user experience. It's particularly useful for presenting articles, blog posts, and other text-heavy content. By applying the appropriate properties, you can customize the column count, gap, rules, and spanning to create visually appealing and well-structured multi-column layouts.

This is applied directly to the element containing the text;

To use the multi-column layout, set the number of columns to a value as follows.

column-count: 5;

column-count

The column-count property specifies the number of columns an element should be divided into.

Values

- auto
- number

auto

Default value. The number of columns is determined by other properties, such as column-width

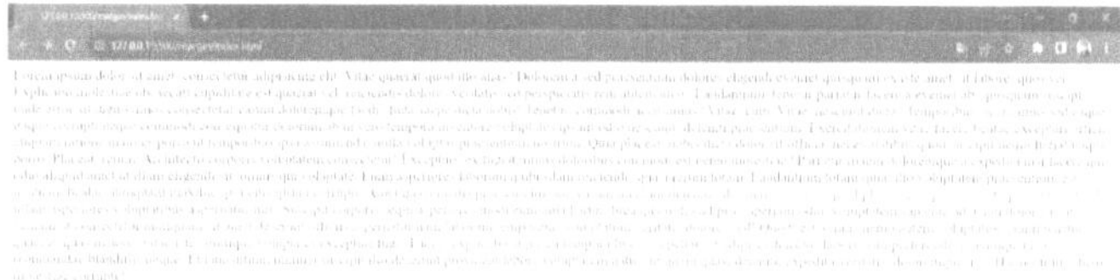

<style>

```css
  .wrapper {
    font-size: 20px;
    column-count: auto;
  }
</style>
<div class="wrapper">
  <p>
    Lorem ipsum dolor sit amet,
consectetur adipisicing elit. Vitae
quaerat quod
    illo alias? Dolorem a sed
praesentium dolores eligendi eveniet
quisquam ex
    iste amet sit labore, quos vel?
Explicabo molestiae obcaecati cupiditate
est
    quaerat vel, reiciendis dolores
veritatis sed perspiciatis rem autem
alias!
    Laudantium, tenetur pariatur facere
a eveniet ab, quisquam suscipit unde
    error sit dignissimos consectetur
earum doloremque facilis fuga saepe
dicta
```

nobis! Tenetur, commodi accusamus? Vitae, eum. Vitae, nesciunt dicta?

Temporibus, accusamus sed eaque itaque corrupti neque commodi consequatur

dolorum ab in vero tempora inventore voluptates ipsum odio nesciunt,

deleniti praesentium. Exercitationem vitae facere beatae excepturi officiis

aliquam ratione maiores porro ut temporibus ipsa assumenda, nulla voluptas

praesentium nostrum. Quia placeat, nobis dicta dolor sit officia,

necessitatibus quod suscipit nemo fugiat itaque porro. Placeat, rerum.

Architecto corporis voluptatem consectetur! Excepturi, ex fugiat minus

doloribus commodi est nemo molestiae? Pariatur magni doloremque a expedita

nisi facere quis odio aliquid amet ut illum eligendi sit, omnis qui voluptate. Enim asperiores laborum quibusdam reiciendis quasi rerum totam.

Laudantium totam quia, illo voluptatem praesentium est magnam beatae numquam

maxime ipsa eius ipsum corrupti! Amet quasi facilis praesentium sunt earum

incidunt deleniti odit, delectus vitae quod placeat nisi possimus itaque omnis id vel ullam asperiores voluptatibus aspernatur iure. Suscipit corporis sequi asperiores modi eum quia harum fuga quam illo adipisci aperiam odio, voluptatem sapiente ad. Cum dolor iste at, veniam ut consectetur numquam sit amet deserunt officiis aspernatur nam laborum temporibus voluptatum veritatis dolores sed! Quod, est, omnis nemo autem voluptatibus nihil tenetur quaerat, quas maiores vitae iste similique voluptates excepturi fuga. Facilis explicabo atque ea tempora libero,

```
      repellat est adipisci delectus
laboriosam perferendis ut numquam, a
      repudiandae blanditiis neque. Et
laudantium minima suscipit illo deserunt
      provident labore voluptatem natus,
ut quam quasi deleniti, expedita
      veritatis, doloremque nisi. Hic
nostrum libero molestiae corrupti?
    </p>
</div>
```

number

The optimum number of columns into which the content of the element should flow

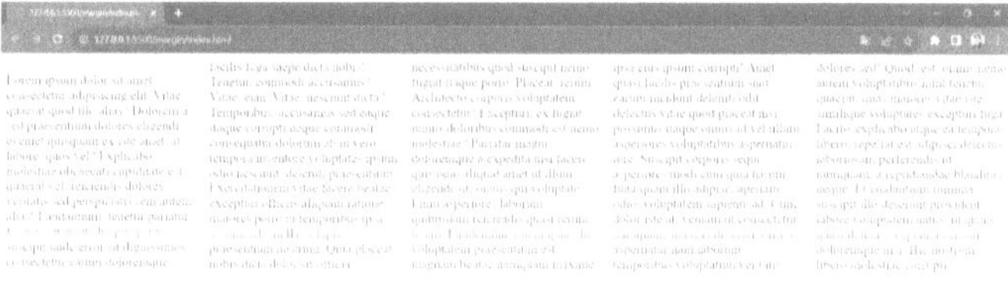

```
.wrapper {
```

```css
    font-size: 20px;
    column-count: 5;
  }
```

column-gap

The column-gap CSS property sets the size of the gap (gutter) between an element's columns.

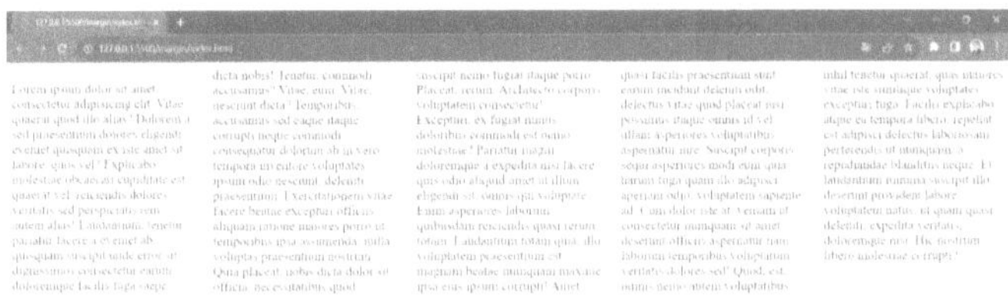

```css
  .wrapper {
    font-size: 20px;
    column-count: 5;
    column-gap: 30px;
  }
```

column-rule

The column-rule property sets the width, style, and color of the rule between columns.

It is a shorthand for the following CSS properties

<column-rule-width> <column-rule-style (required)> <column-rule-color>

column-rule: <column-rule-width> <column-rule-style (required)> <column-rule-color>

Values

- <column-rule-width> <column-rule-style (required)> <column-rule-color>

3px dotted blue

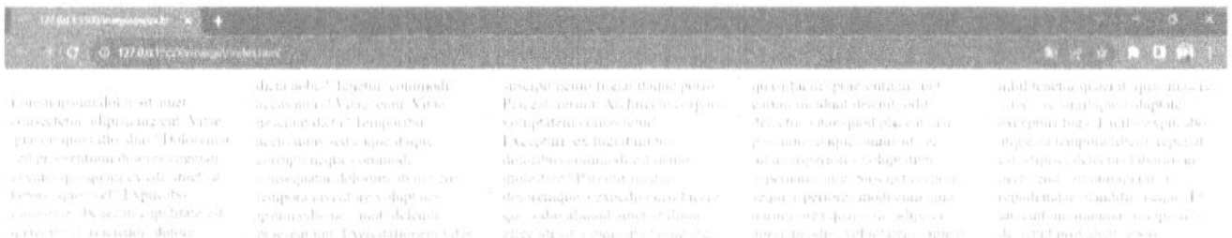

```
.wrapper {
    font-size: 20px;
```

```css
    column-count: 5;
    column-gap: 30px;
    column-rule: 3px dotted blue;
}
```

column-span

The CSS property column-span allows an element to span across all columns if its value is set to all.

Values

- none
- all

none

Default value. The element should span across one column

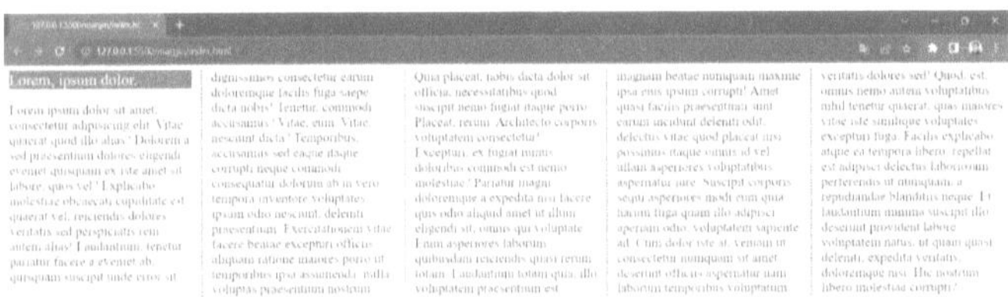

```html
<style>
  .wrapper {
    font-size: 20px;
    column-count: 5;
    column-gap: 30px;
    column-rule: 3px dotted blue;
  }
  .header {
    background-color: darkviolet;
    color: white;
    font-size: 24px;
    column-span: none;
  }
</style>
<div class="wrapper">
  <div class="header">Lorem, ipsum
dolor.</div>
  <p>
    Lorem ipsum dolor sit amet,
consectetur adipisicing elit. Vitae
quaerat quod
    illo alias? Dolorem a sed
praesentium dolores eligendi eveniet
quisquam ex
```

iste amet sit labore, quos vel?
Explicabo molestiae obcaecati cupiditate
est

quaerat vel, reiciendis dolores
veritatis sed perspiciatis rem autem
alias!

Laudantium, tenetur pariatur facere
a eveniet ab, quisquam suscipit unde

error sit dignissimos consectetur
earum doloremque facilis fuga saepe
dicta

nobis! Tenetur, commodi accusamus?
Vitae, eum. Vitae, nesciunt dicta?

Temporibus, accusamus sed eaque
itaque corrupti neque commodi
consequatur

dolorum ab in vero tempora inventore
voluptates ipsum odio nesciunt,

deleniti praesentium. Exercitationem
vitae facere beatae excepturi officiis

aliquam ratione maiores porro ut
temporibus ipsa assumenda, nulla
voluptas

praesentium nostrum. Quia placeat,
nobis dicta dolor sit officia,
necessitatibus quod suscipit nemo
fugiat itaque porro. Placeat, rerum.
Architecto corporis voluptatem
consectetur! Excepturi, ex fugiat minus
doloribus commodi est nemo
molestiae? Pariatur magni doloremque a
expedita
nisi facere quis odio aliquid amet
ut illum eligendi sit, omnis qui
voluptate. Enim asperiores laborum
quibusdam reiciendis quasi rerum totam.
Laudantium totam quia, illo
voluptatem praesentium est magnam beatae
numquam
maxime ipsa eius ipsum corrupti!
Amet quasi facilis praesentium sunt
earum
incidunt deleniti odit, delectus
vitae quod placeat nisi possimus itaque
omnis id vel ullam asperiores
voluptatibus aspernatur iure. Suscipit

corporis sequi asperiores modi eum quia harum fuga quam illo adipisci aperiam odio, voluptatem sapiente ad. Cum dolor iste at, veniam ut consectetur numquam sit amet deserunt officiis aspernatur nam laborum temporibus voluptatum veritatis dolores sed! Quod, est, omnis nemo autem voluptatibus nihil tenetur quaerat, quas maiores vitae iste similique voluptates excepturi fuga. Facilis explicabo atque ea tempora libero, repellat est adipisci delectus laboriosam perferendis ut numquam, a repudiandae blanditiis neque. Et laudantium minima suscipit illo deserunt provident labore voluptatem natus, ut quam quasi deleniti, expedita veritatis, doloremque nisi. Hic nostrum libero molestiae corrupti?
  </p>
</div>

all

The element should span across all columns

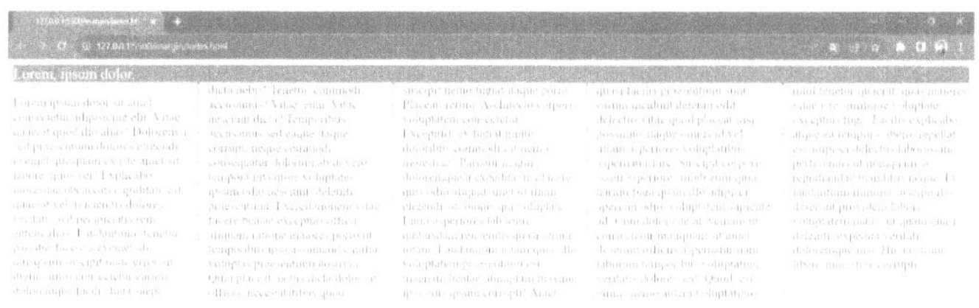

```css
.header {
  background-color: darkviolet;
  color: white;
  font-size: 24px;
  column-span: all;
}
```

column-fill

The CSS property column-fill controls how the content of an element is balanced when it is split into columns.

Values

- balance
- auto

balance

Content is equally divided between columns.

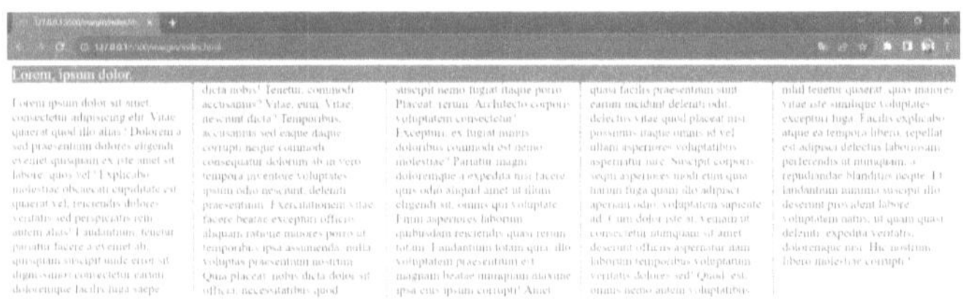

```css
.wrapper {
  font-size: 20px;
  column-count: 5;
  column-gap: 30px;
  column-rule: 3px dotted blue;
  column-fill: balance;
}
```

auto

Columns are filled sequentially.

```css
.wrapper {
  font-size: 20px;
  column-count: 5;
  column-gap: 30px;
  column-rule: 3px dotted blue;
  column-fill: auto;
}
```

Let's define a fixed height for the container and check again

balance

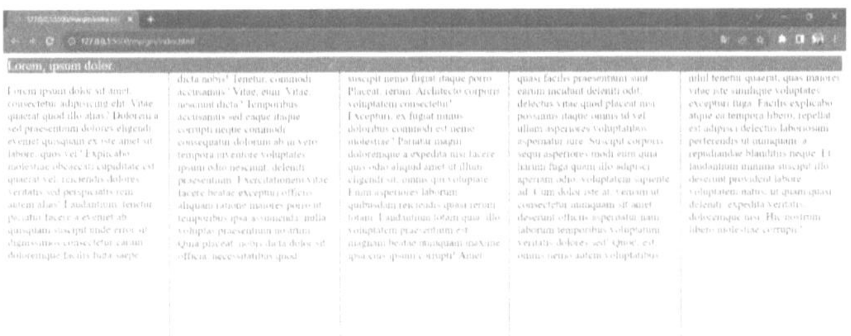

```css
.wrapper {
  font-size: 20px;
  column-count: 5;
  column-gap: 30px;
  column-rule: 3px dotted blue;
  height: 500px;
  column-fill: balance;
}
```

auto

```css
.wrapper {
  font-size: 20px;
  column-count: 5;
  column-gap: 30px;
  column-rule: 3px dotted blue;
  height: 500px;
  column-fill: auto;
}
```

Column Breaks

CSS column breaks are properties that allow you to control how content is divided and displayed in multi-column layouts. They specify where columns should break, whether content should be forced to a

new column or page, and how to handle
column-spanning elements.

break-before

The break-before property determines whether a page
break, a column break or a region break should occur
before the specified element.

Values

- auto
- avoid
- always
- all
- avoid-page
- page
- avoid-column
- column

avoid

Avoid a page/column/region break before the element

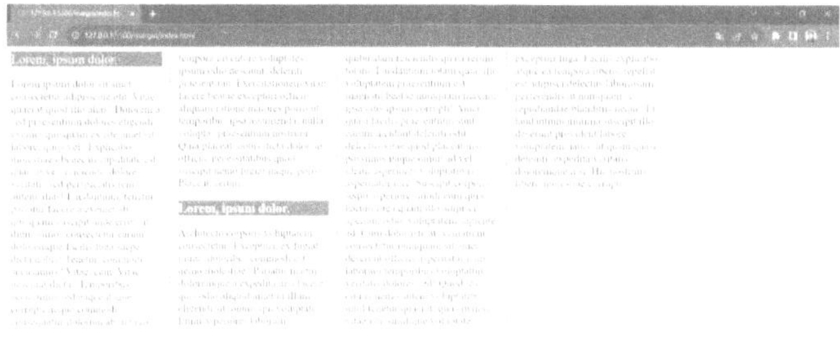

```css
<style>
  .wrapper {
    font-size: 20px;
    column-count: 5;
    column-gap: 30px;
    column-rule: 3px dotted blue;
    height: 500px;
    column-fill: auto;
  }
  .header {
    background-color: darkviolet;
    color: white;
    font-size: 24px;
    column-span: none;
  }
  .title-break {
```

```css
    background-color: darkviolet;
    color: white;
    font-size: 24px;
    break-before: avoid;
  }
```
```html
</style>
<div class="wrapper">
  <div class="header">Lorem, ipsum
dolor.</div>
  <p>
    Lorem ipsum dolor sit amet,
consectetur adipisicing elit. Vitae
quaerat quod
    illo alias? Dolorem a sed
praesentium dolores eligendi eveniet
quisquam ex
    iste amet sit labore, quos vel?
Explicabo molestiae obcaecati cupiditate
est
    quaerat vel, reiciendis dolores
veritatis sed perspiciatis rem autem
alias!
    Laudantium, tenetur pariatur facere
a eveniet ab, quisquam suscipit unde
```

error sit dignissimos consectetur earum doloremque facilis fuga saepe dicta

nobis! Tenetur, commodi accusamus? Vitae, eum. Vitae, nesciunt dicta?

Temporibus, accusamus sed eaque itaque corrupti neque commodi consequatur

dolorum ab in vero tempora inventore voluptates ipsum odio nesciunt,

deleniti praesentium. Exercitationem vitae facere beatae excepturi officiis

aliquam ratione maiores porro ut temporibus ipsa assumenda, nulla voluptas

praesentium nostrum. Quia placeat, nobis dicta dolor sit officia,

necessitatibus quod suscipit nemo fugiat itaque porro. Placeat, rerum.

<h2 class="title-break">Lorem, ipsum dolor.</h2>

Architecto corporis voluptatem consectetur! Excepturi, ex fugiat minus doloribus commodi est nemo molestiae? Pariatur magni doloremque a expedita nisi facere quis odio aliquid amet ut illum eligendi sit, omnis qui voluptate. Enim asperiores laborum quibusdam reiciendis quasi rerum totam. Laudantium totam quia, illo voluptatem praesentium est magnam beatae numquam maxime ipsa eius ipsum corrupti! Amet quasi facilis praesentium sunt earum incidunt deleniti odit, delectus vitae quod placeat nisi possimus itaque omnis id vel ullam asperiores voluptatibus aspernatur iure. Suscipit corporis sequi asperiores modi eum quia harum fuga quam illo adipisci aperiam odio, voluptatem sapiente ad. Cum dolor iste at, veniam ut consectetur numquam sit amet deserunt officiis aspernatur nam laborum

        temporibus voluptatum veritatis
dolores sed! Quod, est, omnis nemo autem
      voluptatibus nihil tenetur quaerat,
quas maiores vitae iste similique
      voluptates excepturi fuga. Facilis
explicabo atque ea tempora libero,
      repellat est adipisci delectus
laboriosam perferendis ut numquam, a
      repudiandae blanditiis neque. Et
laudantium minima suscipit illo deserunt
      provident labore voluptatem natus,
ut quam quasi deleniti, expedita
      veritatis, doloremque nisi. Hic
nostrum libero molestiae corrupti?
  </p>
</div>

column

Always insert a column-break before the element

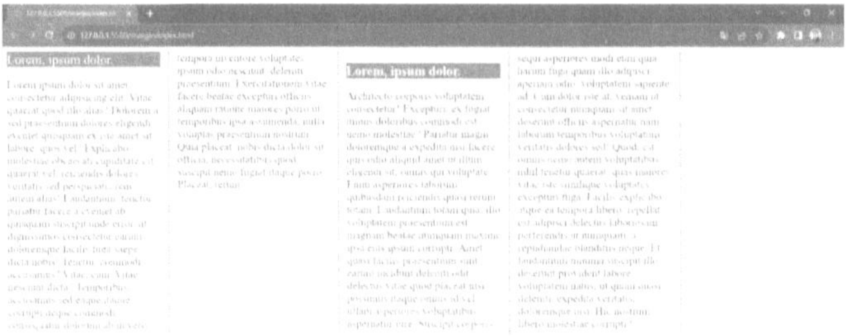

```css
.title-break {
  background-color: darkviolet;
  color: white;
  font-size: 24px;
  break-before: column;
}
```

Conclusion

Congratulations! You have read the book "Responsive Layouts: Flex, Grid and Multi-Column". You now know everything about the most commonly used responsive layouts in CSS.

I am very grateful for the information you learned in this book. This book served more as a reference book explaining all the possible properties and how to use them, but you still need more practice.

I would encourage you to apply what you've learned to real projects to get a better understanding of how all the information you've learned here works.

Good luck!

Media Attribution

Gradient geometric background

Image by pikisuperstar on Freepik

Don't miss out!

Receive an email when Abdelfattah Ragab publishes a new book. It's free and without obligation.

Also by Abdelfattah Ragab

Angular Portfolio App Development
As you have just completed studying CSS layouts I will recommend you to create an online portfolio for you and practice what you have already learned.

In **"Angular Portfolio App Development"** you will learn how to create an online portfolio app to showcase your skills to the world and your potential employers.

About the Author

Abdelfattah Ragab is a professional software developer with more than 20 years of experience. https://abdelfattah-ragab.com

About the Publisher

Abdelfattah Ragab is a highly qualified and experienced software developer with over 20 years of experience in the industry. Specializing in front-end development, Abdelfattah Ragab has a deep understanding of Angular, JavaScript, TypeScript, HTML and CSS. Read more at https://abdelfattah-ragab.com